# KEYS TO GREAT ENLIGHTENMENT

# KEYS TO GREAT ENLIGHTENMENT

COMMENTARIES ON GESHE LANGRI TANGPA'S
*Eight Verses on Thought Training* & TOGMEY ZANGPO'S
*The Thirty-Seven Bodhisattva Practices*

By Geshe Tsultim Gyeltsen

Based on an Oral Translation by Losang Gyaltsen

THUBTEN DHARGYE LING PUBLICATIONS

Thubten Dhargye Ling Archive
P.O. Box 90665 • Long Beach, California 90809 • www.tdling.com

Third Edition for free distribution
First Published by Thubten Dhargye Ling Publications 1989
Second Edition Wisdom Publications under title
*Compassion: The Key to Great Awakening*, 1997

ISBN 0-9623421-0-6

Original commentary translated by Losang Gyaltsen

*The Thirty-seven Bodhisattva Practices* By Togmey Zangpo
Translated by Alexander Berzin and Sharpa Tulku with Jonathan Landaw and
Khamlung Tulku based on an explanation by Geshe Ngawang Dhargyey
Originally published as part of *The Thirty-Seven Practices of All Buddha's Sons* and
*The Prayer of the Virtuous Beginning, Middle, and End* .
Dharamsala, India: Library of Tibetan Works & Archives, 1973.

*Eight Verses on Thought Training* By Geshe Langri Tangpa
From Meditation on 1000-Armed Chenrezig
Compiled by Lama Zopa Rinpoche

*Cover Art:*
Painting of Atisha. From a photograph by Matthieu Ricard, Shechen Archives.
Himalayan Art Resources website • www.himalayanart.org
Front cover background design with kind permission from Robert Beer. From
*The Encyclopedia of Tibetan Symbols and Motifs*; Shambhala Publications, 1999.
Back cover photo by Don Farber

Cover & Book design by Gopa & Ted2, Inc. • Line Art by Andy Weber

# Dedication

*To His Holiness the Fourteenth Dalai Lama of Tibet*
*and all the Holy Masters of the Buddhadharma—*
*may they have long and healthy lives.*

*To the Teachings of the Buddha—*
*may they endure for a very long time.*

*To the members of the Sangha community—*
*may they abide in pure morality, be free of any schism,*
*and succeed in their studies and contemplations.*

*To all beings—*
*may they be free from suffering and*
*may they attain Great Enlightenment.*

*To all the nations of the world—*
*may they be free from illness,*
*famine, war and conflicts.*

*May lasting peace prevail and endure forever.*

*Shakyamuni Buddha*

# Table of Contents

# Acknowledgments

Keys to Great Enlightenment is based on two meditation courses given by Venerable Geshe Tsultim Gyeltsen to the students of Thubten Dhargye Ling as commentaries on the classical root texts: *Eight Verses on Thought Training* by Geshe Langri Tangpa and *The Thirty-Seven Bodhisattva Practices* by the bodhisattva Togmey Zangpo. The book first appeared as *Keys to Great Enlightenment* (Los Angeles: Thubten Dhargye Ling, 1989). The second edition was published by Wisdom Publications under the title *Compassion: the Key to Great Awakening* in honor of His Holiness the Dalai Lama's visit to Los Angeles, sponsored by Thubten Dhargye Ling, in June 1997. This latest edition has been published by Thubten Dhargye Ling Archive in honor of His Holiness the Dalai Lama's September 2006 visit to Los Angeles, also sponsored by Thubten Dhargye Ling. This book has been made available for free distribution, in the belief that the dharma should be accessible by all.

The successful completion of the work has depended upon the efforts of many individuals. Our most sincere thanks are extended first of all to Losang Gyaltsen for contributing his wonderful skill and dedication in translating the author's oral teachings from Tibetan into English during the original meditation courses. Heartfelt thanks are also due to John Dunne for contributing the English translations of the two root texts for the first edition.

The oral commentaries were transcribed and revised by Gary

Schlageter and Karen Gudmundsson. Under the supervision of Robert Stone, these working texts were then proofread and edited with the help of Pat Aiello, Paul McClelland, Nancy Nason and others. Revised drafts were checked with Geshe Gyeltsen for clarification and corrections. Printing of the first edition was carried out by Pat and Gabriel Aiello, whose generosity and assistance are deeply appreciated. We also wish to express our appreciation to the staff at Wisdom Publications for providing a further round of editorial revisions for the second edition, and for allowing this book to reach an even wider audience.

This third edition was published under the supervision of Venerable Geshe Tsultim Gyeltsen with additional editing and production by Rebecca McClen Novick. We extend our thanks to Dr. Nick Ribush for his sound advice, to Gopa & Ted2, Inc. for their thoughtful design, and to Annie McCormack for her assistance with the project and for all her efforts on behalf of Thubten Dhargye Ling. We also extend our deep appreciation to Doren Harper whose dedication to the archive project has made it possible to publish and distribute these books free of charge.

Above all, our sincere gratitude goes to the author of these teachings, Venerable Geshe Tsultim Gyeltsen, for his kindness in giving the oral commentaries and for his supervision of the project. May this book fulfill its purpose in providing students interested in Buddhism with practical instructions for engaging in the bodhisattva path.

*Students of Thubten Dhargye Ling*

# Preface

ALL PEOPLE WISH FOR GREAT HAPPINESS and joy, but for a number of reasons we suffer from recurrent problems, pain, frustration and anguish. Even though we have modern conveniences that make our lives temporarily easier, many of us often focus on immediate pleasure and are unaware of the cost and resultant suffering of what we imagined would bring us happiness. For example, when buying a new house one usually experiences joy at first. But soon this joy can turn to anxiety about the mortgage payments, burglaries and costly repairs. This example illustrates the truth about most objects of enjoyment in our lives. It is common that an object cultivated for happiness turns instead into suffering and problems.

To obtain true happiness, we actually need to destroy the cause of suffering. Two thousand five hundred years ago, Shakyamuni Buddha set forth methods for finding true peace and complete freedom. These methods are based on compassion and wisdom, and benefit both the people practicing them and those who come into contact with them.

The meditations and practices described in the commentaries on the *Eight Verses on Thought Training* and the *Thirty-Seven Bodhisattva Practices* that Venerable Geshe Tsultim Gyeltsen so generously provides describe the two main actions (collecting merit and purifying negativities) that are necessary to achieve lasting peace and happiness.

The *Eight Verses on Thought Training* are simple but quite profound. They emphasize day-to-day activities which form a focus for bringing about positive thought transformation. Some of the topics in the *Eight Verses* include: seeking enlightenment to benefit others and cherishing others, seeing others as supreme, preventing delusions, holding cherishing difficult people, accepting defeat, and regarding those who harm us as teachers.

The second commentary, on the *Thirty-Seven Bodhisattva Practices*, describes the actual practices of a bodhisattva who is on the path to great enlightenment. By emulating their activities, our negativities can become purified and we can accumulate merit. We then become more like bodhisattvas and we eventually become bodhisattvas.

We can put these texts into practice today. With continuous study and application of what we learn, we will replace unrewarding selfish ways of existence with enlightened thoughts, speech and actions based on compassion and love for others. The resulting benefit to ourselves and to others is real.

The beneficial results of the practice will not necessarily be immediately visible, but like water dripping on a rock, these positive actions will leave their mark of increased peace and tranquility. We thank Venerable Geshe Gyeltsen for presenting these commentaries in a practical way. Through his own example, he is enabling us to achieve lasting happiness for ourselves and others.

With the wish that all readers of this book derive as much benefit from these commentaries as we have.

*Students of Thubten Dhargye Ling*

# Introduction

THERE ARE TWO MAIN THINGS one must do to become a fully enlightened buddha for the benefit of all sentient beings. These are to purify all one's negativities and to collect the necessary merit. To do this, one has to first cultivate relative and ultimate bodhicitta. Relative bodhicitta is the aspiration to attain great enlightenment for the benefit of all living beings. Ultimate bodhicitta is the experiential realization that all things are empty of inherent self-existence. These two types of bodhicitta unlock the door to the Mahayana path.

In order to obtain these two types of bodhicitta, one needs the proper teaching. The purpose of this book is to guide students in first developing bodhicitta and then achieving great enlightenment.

The commentary on the *Eight Verses on Thought Training* explains the methods for developing the two bodhicittas. After one has properly achieved bodhicitta, one needs to engage in the actions of the bodhisattvas. Therefore, the commentary on the *Thirty-Seven Bodhisattva Practices* focuses on how to become a bodhisattva by practicing the thirty-seven verses set forth in the text.

After repeated requests from my students, I gave commentaries on these most precious root texts in 1988. I am grateful to Losang Gyaltsen, a very qualified translator, for his translation of my teaching of these texts from Tibetan into English.

After being on retreats with me, students requested that the teachings be made available for study. I felt that these teachings would not only benefit the students from the course, but would benefit anyone sincerely interested in studying dharma.

I encourage all serious students to read these commentaries slowly. Think about what is being taught, and then genuinely take the time to contemplate the meaning. Next, meditate, so that the true meaning of the words becomes experiential for you. In addition, check with your own teacher to receive additional explanation on these subjects. This will enable you to internalize the meaning of both texts.

Whoever truly wants to help other sentient beings without discrimination must attain buddhahood. To do this, one must complete all the actions of the bodhisattvas. One must become a bodhisattva. This requires bodhicitta. Bodhicitta is the altruistic and compassionate aspiration to attain enlightenment for the benefit of all sentient beings. So, the practices that develop bodhicitta are the keys that unlock the doors to the bodhisattva path and all that follows. The two bodhicittas are the keys for both the Sutra and the Tantra paths.

Whoever wishes to enter the mansion house of the Mahayana Sutras and Tantras will need to receive the keys of bodhicitta and the bodhisattva deeds. May you swiftly achieve both of these for the benefit of all sentient beings.

*Geshe Tsultim Gyeltsen*
*Thubten Dhargye Ling*

# ▪ PART ONE: *The Preliminaries*

Preparation for Practice

Graduated Path to Enlightenment
and Levels of Attainment

*Atisha*

# ⠿ Preparation for Practice

## MOTIVATION FOR STUDYING DHARMA

TO ACHIEVE HAPPINESS both for ourselves and for all other beings, we need to practice dharma. To have a sound practice, we need to understand that the practice of dharma is relevant both to our personal conduct and to our relationships with other sentient beings. The practice of dharma must become a very important activity in our life.

The initial step is to develop proper motivation. This produces a proper practice session. The great Lama Tsongkhapa said that if our mind is kind or noble, so will be our path and the teachings. We need to correctly generate a sincere wish to attain great enlightenment in order to benefit all sentient beings. Our effort should be to make ourself a Mahayana being.

Our topic is the quintessence of the eighty-four thousand teachings of the Buddha. It is the system of the supreme vehicle (*yana*), which helps the fortunate practitioner on his way toward enlightenment. It is one of the most supreme paths, highly admired by the great beings like Maitreya, Manjushri, and a great many other bodhisattvas. It was introduced by great trailblazers such as Aryas Asanga and Nagarjuna, and is the heart essence of the practices of the great Atisha and Lama Tsongkhapa. In short, it is the essence of the graduated path to enlightenment or lam-rim.

## SUFFERING AND THE CAUSE OF SUFFERING

Just as we detest suffering, so do all other sentient beings. Since we detest suffering, it is our duty to eradicate our present suffering and also to prevent the suffering that might happen in our future lives.

If suffering could be eradicated by means of wealth alone, then rich people should be totally happy. But that is not necessarily the case. In fact, we know that they may suffer as much or more than we do. To illustrate this point, Nagarjuna says in *Letter to a Friend* (*Suhrillekha*) that there are some *nagas* who have many heads. The more heads they have, the more suffering they endure. Similarly, external wealth only causes more suffering. The more we have, the more suffering we are likely to face, and the more troubles we attract. In order to remove suffering totally from our life or our being, we must remove its cause.

What is the cause of suffering? There are two causes: actions (*karma*), and negative mental states (*kleshas*). When we talk about actions and negative mental states, we are referring to our own actions and our own negative mental states that need to be conquered. We cannot conquer somebody else's. Rather, we should conquer our own—that goal is within our means. To remove our suffering, we have to remove the negative mental states from our mind. Just saying mantras or prayers will not work. What we need to do is to sit down and meditate.

## THE METHOD FOR FREEDOM
## FROM SUFFERING

We cannot eliminate our suffering by means of material objects. We have to gain freedom from a different source. The means by which we can achieve total freedom from all suffering—from all our present and future suffering, as well as all the suffering of other sentient beings— is through dharma practice, through meditation.

How do we meditate? This is a skill we need to learn. Vasubandhu advises us that, "One should keep very pure moral conduct and be very well-informed." So, as well as maintaining pure morality, we must become well-informed. We do this by receiving teachings from the lamas and studying the texts which illuminate the subject matter. We need good information and good teachings because without them we cannot properly conduct our meditation. If we have not heard anything about a subject, we cannot understand it. To emphasize this point, the great Sakya Pandita said, "One who is trying to meditate without proper learning is like an armless person trying to climb a rock." We need sound learning, and the way to obtain it is by thorough study.

## How to Extract the Essence of the Dharma Teachings

When we learn a new concept, we should not just stop there. Rather, once we have understood its meaning, we should think about it repeatedly until it becomes a part of our mind. Only then will our meditation be successful. So we need to follow this procedure: first, gain understanding by listening and studying; second, think repeatedly about what we have heard; third, meditate single-pointedly on the concept. These are the three wisdoms: the wisdom of learning, the wisdom of thinking, and the wisdom of meditation. These come consecutively, and because studying and listening to the dharma is the first step, it is the foundation for the other two and thus becomes very important for our personal life.

Even if we have received a certain teaching once or twice, we should not be complacent about hearing it again. Instead, we should try to receive teachings on dharma subjects as many times as possible and then meditate on them. I know some monks who take teachings on certain texts as many as twenty or thirty times and, even then, would like to receive more teachings. So, the more times we hear teachings, the better it is for our understanding. Many lamas say that if you attend teachings frequently, even on the same subject, you may not hear anything new, but you will understand something new.

We need to remember that every time we attend a teaching we may gain new understanding, even if we are already familiar with the subject. That is a gift from our teachers. Their advice is filled with blessings. Any time we hear a teaching, we can learn some new way to understand it, to adapt it and make it a part of our life, and to bridge the distance between the teachings and our mind. We should not listen to the teaching as separate from ourselves. Instead, we should try to blend the teaching and its message with our mind. Let them blend into each other, let them go together—that should be our goal. If our mind and the teaching go in two different directions, then even though the teaching may be extremely inspirational or blessed, we will not receive any lasting benefit.

## REGARDING THE TEACHINGS AS A MIRROR

We should regard the teachings as a mirror in which we check our actions. Whenever we study or look deeply into dharma, we should be able to see clearly the reflection of our improper behavior and improper thought.

When we view our bad behavior in the mirror of the dharma, we should not get upset. We should remember that our purpose in studying dharma is to expose and uproot our negative mental states. Still sometimes, when we attend a teaching, we may regard some part of it as a harsh criticism of our lives or as a view with which we do not agree. We may even get upset, but that is not the way it should be. There is a Tibetan proverb which illustrates this point, and I would like to share it with you. During one discourse, the lama advised a group of students not to kill lice. But one student was very fond of killing lice, so he did not like that teaching. In fact, it upset him very much. That night when he returned to his home, he was still upset. So, he got hold of a louse and he said, "Now bring your lama here to protect you!" The point is that the student lacked the ability to use the mirror of the dharma to check his actions. Upon hearing the teachings, he should have been able to acknowledge his own mistakes and he should have resolved to learn how to stop himself from killing in the future. He should have been able to make a strong determination not to kill.

Let's remember that whenever we hear or study dharma, we should make note of the things we should learn, as well as the ways we can implement them. The important thing is to use the dharma like a mirror. Just as we look in the mirror in the morning for any sign of a black spot on our face, we can use the mirror of the dharma to find the black spots in our minds or actions. Once we find the black spots, we can remove them. For that reason, we compare the dharma to the mirror.

The key point is to have the correct motivation when we listen to a teaching or study dharma. Once we adopt the correct motivation, listening and study will be easy. Please keep the proper motivation in your mind at all times.

## THE QUALITIES OF THOSE ATTENDING A TEACHING

We need to discuss the attitude with which we should attend the teachings. The lam-rim teachings discuss the qualifications of the master as well as the students.

The teacher should not only have an intellectual grasp of the subject, but, more importantly, the teacher should be practicing the teaching in his or her own life.

The teacher should have the following ten qualities: 1) well-composed behavior; 2) a peaceful mind due to single-pointed concentration; 3) a peaceful mind due to discriminating wisdom; 4) excellent knowledge; 5) enthusiasm; 6) complete training in the scriptures; 7) understanding of emptiness, or *shunyata*; 8) skill in presenting the dharma; 9) compassion for the students; and 10) sustained patience.

## The Qualifications of the Listener

We have already discussed the motivation with which we should attend the teachings. We need to have a proper attitude. The three elements of the correct attitude are proper motivation, attentiveness, and the ability to retain whatever we have received.

In addition, we should approach the teachings, as well as our daily life and daily practice, with the six intentions discussed in the *Lam-Rim Chenmo*. These six intentions are as follows: 1) to regard ourselves as being seriously ill with an illness caused by many negative mental states; 2) to seek a good doctor who can cure us of our illness—our negative mental states; 3) to regard the teachings as a pill or medication—to recognize that even though we may have found a skilful doctor, we can be cured only by the medication—and the teaching itself as the true antidote for our illness; 4) to hold dharma in high esteem, just as the patient would value the medication he or she takes; 5) to regard ourselves as chronic patients who must continue the medication program in order to be cured, to persist and be consistent in our daily practice, and always to revere the teachings and the teachers; 6) to be determined to stay on course in our dharma practice, to decide every single morning to maintain our practice according to the teachings we have received.

# Graduated Path to Enlightenment and Levels of Attainment

THE LAM-RIM TEACHES US that rebirth as a human is invaluable because of its freedoms and endowments, but is difficult to obtain and easy to lose. The lam-rim also teaches about impermanence and death. Following this are the teachings on the law of cause and effect or karma, on the suffering of the three lower realms, on taking refuge, and so on.

How can we achieve the deepest meaning in this life? We need to find some activity that gives meaning. The essence we can extract from life is divided into three levels of achievement: initial, medium, and highest.

## INITIAL ATTAINMENT

If we have the initial level of achievement or attainment as our goal, we are assured of being reborn in one of the three fortunate realms of happiness: the *deva* (celestial-god) realm, the *asura* (demi-god) realm, or the human being realm. We reach this initial attainment through dharma works or practices. To do this, we need to abstain from the ten non-virtuous activities, and to engage in the excellent moral conduct of the ten virtuous deeds. The cultivation of morality should not just be for a day or two, or a month or so, but should be persistent and continue. We should keep a lifelong morality.

Additionally, this morality has to be supported by the six perfections, or *paramitas*. If we create within ourselves the qualities of a very good person, then we will receive at least a minimal benefit from this human rebirth. Not only should we support morality with the six *paramitas*, but we must also link it with pure prayer or pure dedication. This does not mean a single dedication for an entire life; we mean that every prayer or session, whether an hour long or only a few minutes, should conclude with a prayer of dedication. To reach this level of achievement, we need to cultivate the properties of a good person, a person of proper character.

We achieve this attainment through realization of key topics set forth in the graduated path to enlightenment (lam-rim). These topics include: 1) guru devotion; 2) precious human rebirth and the difficulty of obtaining it; 3) death and impermanence; 4) certainty of death; 5) uncertainty of the time of death; 6) what actually helps at the time of death; 7) types of rebirths; 8) refuge; 9) karma or the law of cause and effect; 10) ten types of karmic actions; 11) suffering of being in samsara; 12) dissatisfaction of samsara.

## Guru Devotion

In lam-rim, we introduce the dharma teachings by discussing how to properly cultivate a spiritual master. The section on guru devotion covers three topics: the benefit of cultivating a guru; the loss or disadvantage of not cultivating a guru; and the negative consequences if we antagonize the guru-disciple relationship.

The main idea is that we should regard our guru as a real buddha and try to have immense respect for him or her. This attitude is extremely beneficial for our spiritual development, so we should always remind ourselves of the kindness of our guru. We need to fortify ourselves daily with the good wish: "Not only in this life, but in all my future lives, may I always be in contact with these great Mahayana spiritual masters like the one that I have at this moment."

## PRECIOUS HUMAN REBIRTH

Considering the precious human rebirth with its freedoms and endowments, I would like to quote the great Lama Tsongkhapa, who says that our present human rebirth with its freedoms and endowments is far more valuable than a wish-granting gem. Human rebirth is extremely rare, and it can be enormously meaningful and helpful for us. But if we allow it to go by without living our lives meaningfully, we will not gain any meaningful results and may even have regrets. This human rebirth is adorned with the eight freedoms and ten endowments—if we were to lose it without having achieved anything meaningful in this life, this would be a great loss.

How can we keep this life from becoming empty and meaningless? We need some activity that makes it meaningful. It is dharma work and action that we are discussing here. If we want to attain the minimal benefit of human rebirth, we should at least try to avoid rebirth in the lower realms or the hell realms and make an effort to liberate ourselves from any chance of falling into any of them. That is the least we can do with this human rebirth. But even that is not good enough. We have to permanently close the door to the lower realms and assure ourselves of a rebirth with happiness and prosperity.

## DEATH AND IMPERMANENCE

We also need to deliberate on our own death and on impermanence. This is important because if we fail to reflect on death, then we will thoughtlessly indulge in negative actions.

On the other hand, if we do realize the inevitability of death we will see that many things are not as important as we once thought, and we will learn to set priorities. This will help us to follow the paths that are explained in the teachings.

## CERTAINTY OF DEATH

After understanding the benefits of thinking about death, we need to contemplate death itself and to convince ourselves of the certainty of our own death. Intellectually, we know that we are going to die, but we still try not to think about it. We do need to think about it and to realize that we will die.

## UNCERTAINTY OF THE TIME OF DEATH

We also need to convince ourselves that we never know when we will die, that the time of our death is uncertain. Even though I wake up this morning as a human being, I can never be sure that I will not die by the evening and be reborn as an animal in a place where there is no water, food, or other necessities of life. This fills my whole being with fear and terror. Do I have any assurance that this will not happen to me? We need to think about that. Many of the older students have heard this several times before, but the new ones may not have heard it yet. We must think repeatedly about the uncertainty of the time of our death as the beginning of our dharma practice.

## WHAT ACTUALLY HELPS AT THE TIME OF DEATH

What proves to be most valuable at the moment of death? We need to consider that. Does any of the wealth we have acquired give us any support at that moment? We need to consider that too. Our parents and our friends—are they any help then? The fact is, at the moment of our death, others may share our concern and want to do everything they can to help us, but it is simply beyond them to help at that moment. We start the journey alone and in darkness.

The only friend that can help us at that time is our dharma practice, if we have done any. Our proper dharma practice proves to be our dearest and most unfailing friend. It is not the only thing to go with us, because our negativities follow us too. We have to realize that at the moment of death, nothing is of greater help than our dharma practice. We need to make a firm determination to continue with it throughout our life.

## TYPES OF REBIRTHS

We need to consider where we may go once we leave this life. There are only two possible destinations: either the lower realms of suffering or the higher realms of happiness. Of these two possibilities, we are most likely to go to the lower realms. The reason for this is that the cause of rebirth in the lower realms is our own negative thoughts and actions. We do not need to learn negative thoughts and actions from anyone else. We learn them automatically or instinctively, and as a result, we are closer to the lower realms. On the other hand, the cause of rebirth in the higher realms is the practice of pure morality, patience, and so on. These practices require much effort and hard work from us right now. We need to think, "How would it be for me if I were in one of those lower realms? Would I be able to tolerate the unbearable sufferings I would experience in those realms?" We also need to ask ourselves, "Can anybody help me out of that situation, or not? Is there anything that can give me refuge?"

## REFUGE

Definitely, there is a refuge. We can be helped by the Buddha, the Dharma, and the Sangha. Taking refuge in these three is very important.

Many of us feel that if we have taken refuge once it is sufficient, but that is not true. We should try to take refuge as often as possible. The more times each day we can go for refuge the better. What distinguishes whether or not we are Buddhists is the presence of the proper refuge in our minds. If we want to be true Buddhists, then we need to take proper refuge in a pure or proper manner each day. Moreover, taking refuge is the foundation for all of the higher Buddhist vows, including the pratimoksha vows—the vows of monks and nuns (*bhikshus* and *bhikshunis*)—the bodhisattva vows and the tantric vows. To receive any of these three higher vows, we must first take refuge to build the foundation. Moreover, when we are to receive an initiation such as that of Avalokiteshvara, this also begins with taking refuge. Again, refuge is the foundation. Therefore, taking refuge is very important for all of us.

What are the objects of refuge? There are three: the Buddha, the Dharma, and the Sangha. The primary refuge is the entire community of buddhas. The Buddha refuge also includes all of our teachers who teach us the unmistaken path and its stages.

The Dharma refuge has two aspects: first, the true Dharma refuge, which is the noble path and insights and the actual freedom from all negativities. These qualities abide in the minds of all the buddhas. The second aspect is the relative dharma refuge, which are the written scriptural texts and the written teachings of the buddhas. It is very helpful if we treat the relative dharma refuge, the texts, as the true Dharma refuge. We should have great respect for our dharma books. We should not misuse them by leaving them on the bare ground, or use them as a cushion to sit on. If we do any of those things, it shows a great disrespect towards the teachings and becomes a heavy negativity.

The Sangha refuge—the supreme community—includes the bodhisattvas, the shravakas, the pratyekabuddhas, the dakas and dakinis, and all the dharmapalas who have attained the arya or the transcendental path.

We need to understand that if we take refuge in the Buddha, the Dharma, and the Sangha, they will not fail us. We need to understand the infallibility of that refuge. Not only are they capable of giving us refuge, but they are worthy of being our refuge. For instance, the Buddha is totally free from fear and can relieve others of fear as well. Moreover, he extends his great compassion equally to all beings. If one praises the Buddha and another insults him, the Buddha shows equal compassion to both, and he helps both, whether they benefit him or not—it does not matter. Unlike us, Buddha helps everybody equally. We need to realize that whether or not we receive help is actually up to us. It is beyond any shadow of doubt that Buddha has the power to help us, but he can do so only if we take refuge in him.

## KARMA OR THE LAW
## OF CAUSE AND EFFECT

Taking refuge is not enough. We must also follow the instructions regarding which actions we should take and which actions we should avoid. If we do not, even though we take refuge we will not achieve nirvana or liberation. We need to realize how important the law of karma (cause and effect) is, and that it is the root of all happiness and prosperity. Once we have strong faith in and respect for the law of cause and effect—once we realize that good action brings happiness and negative action brings suffering—we can learn to refrain from negative action and practice only good action.

There is much discussion about karma in the *Lam-rim Chenmo*, but the important thing we need to remember is that the results of every action are certain. Whatever karma we have created, the results are commensurate. This does not mean that every karma bears a result, for there are modifying conditions; we can spoil the seeds. For instance, although we may commit a negative action, we can confess to purify that action and make that seed impotent. Thus, it is said that there is no negative action that cannot be cleansed with the four antidotes, or four opponent powers, of purification.

We must also realize that any action we have committed, whether virtuous or non-virtuous, will keep on multiplying and compounding day after day. Once we realize this, we can learn to purify every negativity we have committed on that day. We cannot simply afford to let it continue, because if we do, even a minute negative action can become huge after some time. We fall into the depth of the negativities if we let a single small one go by. Moreover, we need to recognize that if we haven't committed a particular action—whether a virtuous or non-virtuous one—we will not receive the result or face the consequences. To experience the result, we must commit the action ourselves. For instance, the karma created by Tashi would not bear fruit on Ngödrup, nor would the karma created by Ngödrup bear its results on Tashi. Tashi and Ngödrup are two different people.

## TEN TYPES OF KARMIC ACTIONS

How many types of karma are there? To summarize, there are ten. We can refer to the ten white paths of action and the ten black paths of action. The ten negative paths or the black karmas include three negative actions of the body: killing, stealing, sexual misconduct; four negative actions of speech: lying, slandering, harsh talk, and idle gossip; and three negative actions of the mind: covetousness, ill will and false views. If we have committed any of these ten, we should feel strong remorse or regret for our actions. Also, we should try to refrain from committing such actions in the future. The ten white paths of virtue are the opposites of the ten non-virtuous actions.

## SUFFERING OF BEING IN SAMSARA

After we have some insight into karma, we need to think about the general suffering of being in samsara. The principle disadvantage of being in the vicious cycle of samsara is the uncertainty of our status. We may have a tendency to think that our enemies will always be our enemies and our friends will always be our friends. But this is not so; enemies can easily change into friends, and friends into enemies. In what way does our understanding of uncertainty as a general characteristic of samsara help us? Usually we create a lot of unnecessary karma because we have a fixed idea of enemy as enemy and friend as friend. Because of that we keep on committing negative karma, but once we realize the uncertainty of our status, we create less.

## DISSATISFACTION OF SAMSARA

The next topic is the unsatisfying nature of samsara. Any samsaric pleasure, no matter how much we indulge in it or how much we enjoy it, never truly satisfies us. There is no samsaric pleasure about which we can say, "I haven't experienced that." We have been cycling in samsara from beginningless time. We have been everywhere and have enjoyed every single samsaric happiness. But do we have anything to show for it right now? No. The pleasures are gone.

We also need to think about how being in samsara requires us to lose our body repeatedly. Every time we lose our bodies and our lives we experience tremendous trauma not only for ourselves, but also for our friends, relatives, and everybody who surrounds us during that life. It is the most traumatic experience we go through in our personal life, and we go through this not once, but repeatedly. Why do we repeatedly have to give up the form we have taken for a particular life? Why are we reborn again and trapped again in the vicious cycle of rebirth? Delusion and karma are the causes of samsara, and they are very much present at this moment. Thus, to stop the cycle of repeated rebirth, we must get rid of negative mental states and karma.

Another negative attribute of being in the chain of samsara is the fluctuation of our status. At times we are at the top of cyclic existence and at others we are on the bottom. For instance, one who enjoys the highest life as a human being, such as a king, may after death take rebirth on the glowing iron surface of hell and become indistinguishable from the heat which consumes the body itself—becoming one of the lowest beings imaginable on the surface of hell. Such fluctuations happen in samsara. Anyone—including professors, actors, singers, and the like, who enjoy a huge number of fans and admirers—may fall into the lower realms and undergo excruciating pain and suffering alone. For that reason, the Seventh Dalai Lama, Kelsang Gyatso, wrote in one of his poems to Avalokiteshvara that all the higher ones soon become slaves who are walked upon by everybody. He also wrote that the beautiful physique of the peasant is like the flower of autumn: it soon vanishes. All of our riches are like borrowed ornaments that we may enjoy for a brief moment but then must return. What we need to learn from these messages is that all samsaric things lack meaning or essence. It is best to take this kind of advice very personally, as if given to us alone by the author. If we can receive every teaching in that way, at that level, it works very effectively.

Another of the demerits of samsara is being alone without friends. We might think this is not true. We tend to think, "I have lots of friends—my parents, my relatives, and so on." However, if you think seriously, that is not really so. When we speak of being alone and friendless in samsara, we do not mean throughout our life. Rather, we are specifically referring to life's two crucial moments: birth and death. These are the two hardest times of our existence, and we must go through them alone without the benefit of friends. This is what is meant by the unfriendliness of samsara. Therefore, we should seek out a real friend who can aid and accompany us at that critical moment.

That friend is our dharma practice, and we should cultivate that friendship from now on.

## REVIEW OF THE LAM-RIM TOPICS
## (FOR INITIAL ATTAINMENT)

We started by discussing guru devotion, then went on to the cultivation of the spiritual master, and the disadvantages of being in the vicious cycle of samsara. If we have the realization of the freedom and preciousness of this human rebirth, if we understand the difficulty of obtaining such a rebirth, and more importantly, if we have the realization of impermanence and death—we can reduce our total preoccupation with the pleasures of this life. If we do not, then we can never find the time for dharma practice because we will always have something else to do. So, it is very important for us to work toward becoming less preoccupied with seeking happiness for this life only.

We have also discussed the infallibility of the law of cause and effect, the law of karma, as well as the general and specific suffering of cyclic existence or samsara. Thinking properly on these topics can help us reduce our preoccupation with this life and enable us to achieve a better rebirth. The realization of death helps us to have a very strong desire to renounce samsara. It makes us unwilling to take rebirth within samsara under the influence of karma and negative mental states, and once we have escaped samsara, we can return out of compassion and love for sentient beings. We can return as a bodhisattva.

*Medium Attainment*

If we wish to achieve medium attainment during this human rebirth, which is liberation from samsara (cyclic existence), we need to cultivate and realize the meaning of the following lam-rim meditations: namely, strong renunciation of samsara and realization of emptiness, or shunyata.

First we need to develop a strong renunciation or strong urge to break free from samsara. We can develop such an urge by changing our attitude towards cyclic existence itself, so that we perceive it as a glowing iron surface or as a hot ember. The cyclic existence which we are discussing does not require us to travel to a distant place or even out of our neighborhood, but rather it is present in our every action by which we produce more causes that bind us to this ember-like samsara. We produce more and more causes each and every day, don't we? This cyclic existence is analogous to a hot-iron surface, but we fail to perceive it that way. As it says in the *Lama Chöpa*, we see cyclic existence as a very beautiful park. In the *Lama Chöpa*, we are urged to sever this attitude towards samsara. We have this misconception because we are almost insane. For those who are insane or mentally incapacitated, it is immensely difficult to see even the worst prison as a prison. Under the very strong influence of the three poisonous negative mental states—hatred, attachment, and ignorance—we fail to see cyclic existence as a most dreadful place; instead we see it as something very desirable. What we need to understand is that cyclic existence is very unpleasant to live in. The right conception or right perception of cyclic existence helps develop the urge to remove ourselves from it. For instance, we would not want to live in a dangerous place surrounded by fear for even a single moment. We would want to try and get out of it as soon as we could.

We need to contemplate these concepts because they don't come easily to our mind. With continuous contemplation, we reach a point where we do not wish to stay in cyclic existence at all. When a very sincere, strong urge to be released from cyclic existence comes to our mind, that is the point at which we have developed very strong renunciation. We have a strong wish to get out of cyclic existence, but the wish alone does not deliver us. The final deliverance from cyclic existence can only be achieved through insight into emptiness.

The wisdom of emptiness (*shunyata*) can sever the very root of cyclic existence. We need to understand that without the help of the wisdom that understands emptiness, even if we spend our entire life in meditation, we cannot break free from cyclic existence. There is no way out without the help of the wisdom of emptiness. It is the key tool or weapon with which we can cut the very root of ignorance, and thus cut the root of hatred and attachment which stems from ignorance. Initially we need to develop renunciation and then work toward the development of insight into the wisdom of emptiness.

We can break free from samsara with the help of the wisdom of emptiness. Whenever we develop direct non-conceptual understanding or insight into emptiness from then on we do not create any new causes of rebirth into cyclic existence. In addition, all the karmas that we might have accumulated in the countless number of lives prior to that moment can be effectively eliminated with the help of the newly discovered insight. To substantiate this, I will quote from Aryadeva's *Four Hundred Stanzas of Madhyamaka* (*Catuhshataka*) where he says, "Even a doubt about inherent existence which inclines toward the right conclusion, that alone will tear samsara into pieces." Whenever we successfully put an end to delusive obscurations and successfully obtain liberation for ourselves, then at that moment we have achieved the medium essence of this human birth. Once we are out of samsara, then there is no relapse. We cannot be reborn in samsara. We gain a permanent freedom from cyclic existence, and we are not subject to suffering from then on.

## HIGHEST ATTAINMENT

If we wish to achieve the highest level of attainment during this human rebirth, which is the state of great enlightenment, we need to realize the meaning of the following lam-rim meditations: great com-

passion by either of the two special methods; engaging in the bodhisattva activities, and completing the five paths and the ten bodhisattva
stages (*bhumis*).

We still have some obstacles which need to be overcome, and there
is more to be obtained. What we need to do to enable us to overcome
all the obstacles and achieve the final attainment or achievements, is
to enter into the Mahayana path. As we enter the Mahayana path, the
first step is the development of great compassion (*mahakaruna*). There
are methods or steps that we can follow to help us develop this great
compassion. If one follows the supreme method set forth by the great
Shantideva, one tries to cultivate great compassion by the exchange of
self with others.

If we follow the traditions set forth by the great Maitreya and Arya
Asanga, we need to develop the following seven steps: 1) recognition
of all sentient beings as our mothers; 2) recollection of their kindness;
3) an intention to repay their kindness; 4) cultivating great love
towards all. Contemplation on great love produces 5) great compassion as its result. It comes quite rapidly, arising spontaneously in our
mind. When we have developed great compassion, we become members of the Mahayana family. It is almost like a passport. Further development and familiarization with great compassion produces 6)
exceptional thought. This is exceptional thought in the sense that due
to the strength of our compassion our mind has become more forceful and much stronger. One result of exceptional intention is 7) precious bodhicitta.

The difference between exceptional thought and great compassion
is that with great compassion we have a very strong wish or desire that
all sentient beings be free from suffering, but we do not have the
exceptional sense of responsibility that says, "I will look for the means
to make them free from suffering." At the exceptional thought stage,
we accept that personal responsibility. As a result, if we have managed
to cultivate bodhicitta, then we have truly become a bodhisattva.

The level of attainment to which we aspire determines the resultant attainment which we achieve. Maximum attainment should be our goal because it enables us to truly have the means of bringing the greatest benefit to others and to fulfill our highest personal goals.

Achieving the highest attainment during this lifetime is not beyond our means. However, this task requires us to cultivate the proper outlook and to engage in activities that lead to this result. The following two texts help us to do this. The *Eight Verses on Thought Training* explains clearly how to develop the mind needed to achieve the highest attainment, i.e., the two bodhicittas; and the *Thirty-Seven Bodhisattva Practices* explains the activities in which we must engage in order to become a bodhisattva.

# PART TWO: *Eight Verses on Thought Training*

Root Verses

Commentary

Questions & Answers

*Geshe Langri Tangpa*

# The Root Verses

*With the thought of attaining enlightenment*
*For the welfare of all beings,*
*Who are more precious than a wish-fulfilling jewel,*
*I will constantly practice holding them dear.*

*Whenever I am with others,*
*I will practice seeing myself as the lowest of all*
*And from the very depth of my heart,*
*I will respectfully hold others as supreme.*

*In all actions, I will examine my mind*
*And the moment a disturbing attitude arises,*
*Endangering myself and others,*
*I will firmly confront and avert it.*

*Whenever I meet a person of bad nature*
*Who is overwhelmed by negative energy and intense suffering,*
*I will hold such a rare one dear,*
*As if I had found a precious treasure.*

*When others, out of jealousy,*
*Mistreat me with abuse, slander, and so on,*
*I will practice accepting defeat*
*And offering the victory to them.*

*When someone I have benefited*
*And in whom I have placed great trust*
*Hurts me very badly,*
*I will practice seeing that person as my supreme teacher.*

*In short, I will offer directly and indirectly*
*Every benefit and happiness to all beings, my mothers.*
*I will practice in secret taking upon myself*
*All their harmful actions and sufferings.*

*Without these practices being defiled by the stains of the eight*
    *worldly concerns,*
*By perceiving all phenomena as illusory,*
*I will practice without grasping to release all beings*
*From the bondage of the disturbing, un-subdued mind and karma*

# ⁞ The Commentary on the Root Verses

## HISTORICAL BACKGROUND

IN ACCORDANCE WITH the traditional systems of study at the two great monastic universities of ancient India, Vikramalashila and Nalanda, we start the teaching with a brief talk on the qualities of the author of the text in order to gain greater respect for the teachings. The more we know about the author, the more we can trust the teachings. If we were to discuss the origins of these teachings, we would start with the life of Shakyamuni Buddha, then proceed down to Atisha, Geshe Chekawa, Lama Tsongkhapa, and so on. However, we do not have time to talk about all of these great teachers in detail. Still, we can summarize the origin of these teachings.

The source is Shakyamuni Buddha. He initially developed bodhicitta and acquired the merits of both profound insights and the great deeds for three countless eons, and finally achieved great enlightenment. After Shakyamuni Buddha came the great aryas, Asanga and Nagarjuna, whose deeds are beyond our comprehension. I would highly recommend that you study the lives of these great beings. It would be extremely helpful for your practice. We should be especially grateful to Arya Asanga and Arya Nagarjuna, because they made the teachings of the Mahayana radiate like the sun throughout the world. They are the ones who brought forth the light of the Mahayana practice after the *mahaparinirvana* of Buddha on this earth. Next, there was the great Shantideva. His main work is titled *Bodhicaryavatara* or *Guide to the Bodhisattva Way of Life.* If you refer to that text, you can see what kind of life Shantideva led. Later came Serlingpa, who was the principal authority on the bodhicitta practice teachings of his time. He was the one from whom Atisha received the entire teaching on the precious bodhicitta. He was the holder of the great treasury of the entire teachings (including both wisdom and method) of Shakyamuni Buddha. Atisha is universally admired in both India and Tibet, and he was the founder of the Kadam tradition of Tibetan Buddhism.

These teachings on thought training were passed on unbroken from Shakyamuni Buddha down to the great Atisha. The primary student to whom Atisha passed on this entire teaching was Dromtönpa. He in turn passed it on to his chief students Geshe Potowa, Geshe Sharawa, and Geshe Langri Tangpa. In those days, these teachings were orally transmitted to only a few students. This was because the aim of thought training was to teach the student to learn to accept the sufferings of others as their own and to be totally supportive of others. This was a message that few people were able to believe in. Many of them feared that such teachings would bring more suffering upon themselves. So the teaching was passed on only to those whom the teacher judged to be qualified.

When Geshe Langri Tangpa received these teachings on thought training from Dromtönpa, he believed they were very profound and beyond the thought of ordinary people, and he felt it would be a tremendous loss if they were not preserved. So he recorded the teaching in written form as *Eight Verses on Thought Training.* Years later, after Geshe Langri Tangpa had passed away, Geshe Chekawa found a written version of his *Eight Verses on Thought Training.* Geshe Chekawa was extraordinary in his grasp of the teachings, his practice, his power of listening, and contemplation. He was moved by one verse in particular in the text that states, "I will practice accepting defeat and offering the victory to them [others]." Determined to meet the author of this text, he started to search for him, unaware that Geshe Langri Tangpa had passed away. In a small town near Lhasa, someone informed him of Geshe Langri Tangpa's passing and suggested that he meet Geshe Sharawa instead. This geshe gave him the entire precepts of the teachings on thought training, and Geshe Chekawa wrote the *Seven Point Thought Training* as a commentary to *Eight Verses on Thought Training*. Afterwards, he proclaimed these teachings on thought training "in the market place"—that is, he taught them openly and widely. This practice became very popular, especially among those with chronic diseases like leprosy. Many people wrote about the power and blessedness of these teachings, and the number of people who practiced this method of thought training increased. In Tibet, even though many people may not know the meaning of the thought training teachings, they at least recognize the name of this practice.

## THE GREATNESS OF THE TEACHING

Having discussed the author, we need to discuss the greatness of the teaching itself. This topic is not explained in the *Eight Verses on Thought Training*. Instead, we need to refer to Geshe Chekawa's *Seven Point Thought Training*. In that text, it says that this thought training is like a diamond, in that even its fragments excel every other jewel. So, if we practice even a fragment or a single part of this thought training, we will have greater success than with any other practice. The text also likens thought training to the sun and to a medicinal plant. Just as the sun dispels darkness, the practice of thought training dispels the grasping of the ego from our being, thus freeing us from negative mental states, suffering and the creation of bad karma. Just as the medicinal plant can cure many illnesses, thought training can eliminate suffering and problems that result from self-cherishing. This is the greatness of this practice. Once we understand its value and power, our interest in it will grow, and we will do the practice happily and sincerely.

The name of this type of practice is *lojong* or thought training. The thought training teachings derive from two essential practices which both serve to develop bodhicitta: 1) the exchange of self with others, and 2) tonglen, the practice of giving and receiving. These are actually advanced lam-rim teachings, but when Geshe Langri Tangpa taught thought training, he began at this advanced level because his students already knew that the lam-rim teachings were the foundation of the thought training practice.

## COMMENTARY ON THE ROOT TEXT

### Verse One: Seeking Enlightenment for the Sake of Others and Holding Them Dear

*With the thought of attaining enlightenment*
*For the welfare of all beings,*
*Who are more precious than a wish-fulfilling jewel,*
*I will constantly practice holding them dear.*

If we follow the Tibetan text, it says that sentient beings are far more important than a wish-fulfilling jewel. This is because our achievement of the peerless state of great enlightenment depends on sentient beings. It is said that if we wash the wish-fulfilling jewel three times, polish it three times, hang it on top of a huge banner and ask it for anything, it can provide all our basic needs like food, shelter, or whatever else we ask for. Yet sentient beings are far more precious because their existence enables us to achieve the state of great enlightenment. No such claim can be made for a wish-fulfilling jewel. The key point is that if there were no sentient beings, there would be no individual enlightenment.

Without sentient beings, there is no compassion; without compassion there is no bodhicitta; and without bodhicitta, there is no great enlightenment. Therefore, we say that the kindness of sentient beings and the kindness of the Buddha are equal. We understand the kindness of the Buddha. We know that the Buddha is extremely kind, and we feel grateful to the Buddha because he is the source of all our teachings. He taught the means or techniques of attaining great enlightenment. Without those techniques, enlightenment would not be possible. As an example, even if someone gave us excellent machinery to till the land for growing food, it would be of no use to us if we did not have any land. Similarly, the great Shantideva says in the *Bodhicaryavatara* that sentient beings and the Buddha are equal in terms of our attaining enlightenment. Shantideva states that we have tremendous respect for the buddhas but we have none for sentient beings. What kind of thinking is that?

In the *Seven Point Thought Training*, Geshe Chekawa says that everyone should feel grateful to all sentient beings. Moreover, when we are trying to develop bodhicitta, it is the understanding that all sentient beings have been our mothers that serves as the foundation of the bodhicitta. Great compassion is the root of all the great qualities and great achievements of the Mahayana practices. We develop great compassion in our mind by focusing on sentient beings. Since all our immediate and ultimate happiness and prosperity originates from sentient beings, may we learn to hold them dear.

It would be very helpful, especially for new students, to think about the kindness of other beings in our daily life. We need to think that all our friends, enemies, and strangers are equally kind to us. If we think seriously, we can see that all the food, clothing, and happiness that we have, come directly or indirectly from other sentient beings. We manufacture hardly any of these things ourselves. For instance, when we were born, we had nothing but our naked bodies, and even that we owe to the kindness of our parents. In fact, we have come into this world with nothing. Everything that we have now is due to the kindness of other sentient beings.

Thus, when we say, "May I learn to hold them dear," we do not mean that we should hold their hands all the time, but rather we should understand their needs. We understand that what sentient beings need is happiness and what they detest is suffering. Since we cherish them, we have to look for the means by which we can provide what they need and dispel what they dislike—that should be our personal responsibility. I ask you to do your own study. Imaginatively explore your own ideas, read books, contemplate their meaning, and do whatever you can to increase your understanding of this subject.

### Verse Two: Seeing Others As Supreme

*Whenever I am with others,*
*I will practice seeing myself as the lowest of all*
*And from the very depth of my heart,*
*I will respectfully hold others as supreme.*

This verse is very important for all of us. It advises us that wherever we are and with whomever we associate, we should think of ourselves as the lowest of all, thus developing proper humility and removing our haughtiness or arrogance. If we can hold the lowest position—feel the most humble—we will achieve all of the great qualities and realizations. Most importantly, this will pacify our arrogance. Every day, we need to keep a constant watch over our arrogance and bring it under control.

Arrogance is a barrier to learning, because it prevents us from asking about the things we do not know. It may manifest itself when we are in the presence of our lama and he asks us if we have understood or remembered a teaching, and we have not, but instead we give a false answer or gesture back to the lama that we did understand or remember a teaching. We have a proverb in Tibet that states, "The steel ball of arrogance will bear no grass of knowledge." In our daily life, we can accomplish more if we are humble than if we are not.

Arrogance can prove very dangerous, because it can cause us to disparage our spiritual master. As an example, the great Milarepa had a student named Rechungpa, who made three trips to India. During these trips he had the opportunity to meet many of India's great pundits, including Naropa. When he came back to Tibet, knowing that his lama Milarepa had never made the trip to India and had never met any of those great beings, Rechungpa felt he was more learned and more advanced than his teacher. Milarepa immediately sensed this and knew that for his student's insights to develop further, Rechungpa's arrogance would have to be curbed.

Once when they were going on a trip, Milarepa saw the horn of an animal along the side of the road and asked Rechungpa to pick it up, since it might become useful someday. Rechungpa, of course, had to comply. However, he was not feeling very comfortable about picking up the horn. He thought of Milarepa, "What a discrepancy between his actions—sometimes he acts like he does not have possessiveness for anything, not even for gold and silver, but at other times he is so possessive that he asks me to pick up an abandoned yak horn."

During their trip, they came to a very flat area, without any trees or any other kind of shelter. Milarepa said, "How about staying here? I have a very good reason to stay here for awhile." At first, the weather was good, but all of a sudden, black clouds formed and a terrible storm—with lightning, gale winds and hail—began. Milarepa and Rechungpa were dressed only in cotton clothes, so the hailstones were very painful. When the storm lightened up a little bit, Rechungpa could not find his lama, but he could still hear Milarepa's voice. Looking all around, he finally found the source of the voice. It was coming from the horn! When he peeked through the hole in the horn, he found that Milarepa had not become smaller, nor had the yak horn become bigger. But there was Milarepa inside the horn. And Milarepa said to him, "Oh, my son, if you are equal to your father, then come inside the horn." Rechungpa replied that, of course, he could not. Feeling sorry, he asked for forgiveness. At that moment, Rechungpa lost his arrogance for good.

The other danger of arrogance is that it causes us to belittle or underestimate others. Of course, whenever we belittle somebody it makes them look inferior to us. But we never know where the emanations of the buddhas and bodhisattvas might exist. They do not discriminate regarding the form they might take, appearing as men, women, children, animals, even as inanimate objects. So we cannot determine for sure whether this or that person is a buddha or bodhisattva. If we belittle somebody who is the emanation of our own teacher or the emanation of a buddha or bodhisattva, we commit a very negative action. One of the chief students of Lama Tsongkhapa, Gyaltsab Je, in the commentary *Illumination of the Path to Liberation*, advises us, "During our course of study, we must make sure that we do not use harsh words or belittle anybody because we do not know where the great holy beings are. So we must consider everyone and everything like burning embers hidden under pressed soil. We should remain mindful of this." Often in the sutras, the Buddha said, "Only a person like myself can judge the value of a person, not one person to the next." An ordinary person cannot judge others, only buddhas can.

If we could develop the perception of everything and everyone as pure, we would be able to develop more respect for everybody. This, in turn, would enable us to accumulate much merit. The author, the great Geshe Langri Tangpa, in the third and fourth line of this second verse, prays and wishes from the depths of his heart that we may be able to see all other sentient beings as supreme.

### Verse Three: Preventing Delusions

*In all actions, I will examine my mind*
*And the moment a disturbing attitude arises,*
*Endangering myself and others,*
*I will firmly confront and avert it.*

The third verse refers to "all actions," which are four in number and encompass every activity. Actions are broadly grouped as going quickly, standing, sitting down and sleeping. These actions encompass our physical behavior, our verbal behavior, and our mental behavior—i.e., actions of body, speech and mind. We should monitor every single action of our life very closely. We should not only check what we are about to do, but we should observe the presence of negative mental states or afflictive emotions as they arise in our mental continuum. We need to watch our mind constantly to see if any of these afflictive emotions—like longing, desire, hatred, attachments, jealousy, begrudging, and so on—are arising. If we observe such negative mental states, we should confront them immediately, and forcefully pray, "May I be able to avert them. May I be able to notice the presence of these afflictive emotions, and at the same time may I be able to confront them and reverse them." If we fail to reverse these afflictive emotions at that moment, what is lost? The effect is to bring ourselves and all other beings into potential danger. For instance, if we are with somebody and we become angry, the other person may also become angry; we may end up exchanging harsh words or even fighting.

The result of anger is hatred, which destroys the merits that we have accumulated through much hardship. In a similar manner, if we become driven by extreme longing and desire, we will have hardly any time for anything else. When we become totally obsessed, we will also pull our friends in along with us. These are just a few examples, so please use your own imagination and come up with your own illustrations.

### Verse Four: Cherishing Difficult People

*Whenever I meet a person of bad nature*
*Who is overwhelmed by negative energy and intense suffering,*
*I will hold such a rare one dear,*
*As if I had found a precious treasure.*

This verse could also refer to people afflicted with a contagious disease or a fatal illness. Usually, when we encounter people of bad nature, we try to ignore them instead of cherishing them, and we may advise others to stay away from such persons. We especially try to avoid people who are insane or who have a contagious disease. We keep our distance from them. Even if somebody has a bad body odor, we try to avoid them. We can ask ourselves, "Why do we do that? Why do we want to avoid such types of people?" By doing this, we find that we are influenced by self-cherishing thoughts. We ignore or neglect those people because we hold ourselves too precious to mingle with them, and we fear that our precious self may also get contaminated.

Geshe Langri Tangpa advises us to reverse such action, and says that whenever we meet people who are ill-tempered, bad-mannered, or who have a contagious disease, we should treat them as if we are discovering a great treasure. When we see such people, let us show great joy at finding them and treat them like a treasure, especially if we are practicing *tonglen*. If we truly want to tackle our own self-grasping, these are the tools with which to do it.

We need to treasure these tools. When we do tonglen meditation—especially when we do the meditation on equalizing and exchanging ourself with others—this advice will be invaluable. We need to incorporate these meditations into this practice.

### Verse Five: Accepting Defeat

*When others, out of jealousy,*
*Mistreat me with abuse, slander and so on,*
*I will practice accepting defeat*
*And offering the victory to them.*

This verse is one of the most important parts of this practice. It is the verse that inspired Geshe Chekawa to write the *Seven Point Thought*

*Training.* If we aspire to full enlightenment, we have no choice but to do this practice. We need to learn to offer others the victory, the compliments, whatever is noble and good, and to accept the defeats and losses ourselves. This is the very foundation of the entire bodhisattva practice. If we have bodhicitta, this practice comes automatically. Even in samsaric terms, if we are able to offer the gain and the victory to others, we will prevail in the end; we receive the benefits.

We all know that this practice is not easy. Indeed, it is one of the most difficult practices, but we have to start somewhere. If we start very humbly, then eventually we will be able to do much more. For instance, if we can start by accepting ninety-nine percent of the benefit for ourselves, and giving only one percent to others, we will gradually be able to increase what we can give to others. If we have a sincere interest in this practice, it is possible for us to achieve this result. All the buddhas of the present time and also all the bodhisattvas who are at a very high level of realization had very humble beginnings. This is something that we need to keep in mind at all times.

### Verse Six: Regarding Those Who Harm Us as Teachers

*When someone I have benefited*
*And in whom I have placed great trust*
*Hurts me very badly,*
*I will practice seeing that person as my supreme teacher.*

This particular thought training verse is a difficult practice, but the message is clear. If you develop an interest in the practice, you will find it gets easier. When we treat someone very nicely and provide them with all the care we can give and that person mistreats us in return, we usually regard that person as mean or vile.

At the worldly level, there are bad people who repay good deeds with mistreatment. However, according to Geshe Langri Tangpa, we should regard such a person as the most supreme spiritual teachers or lamas. We can understand the reasoning by thinking about the law of cause and effect. We should be able to understand that what we experience is really the result of our own negative karma.

We have behaved in a similar manner toward other beings in a past life and created this result. We must treat this as a great kindness done to us by this person because it is truly a reflection of the maturation of our own bad karma. If it had not matured in such a manner, it could be far worse in the future. This person has actually been very kind to us by ripening our bad karma. This attitude should enable us to thank the person for behaving in such a manner. In his *Bodhicaryavatara* (*Guide to the Bodhisattva Way of Life*), Shantideva says, "Your enemy is the true provider of all your virtue."

### Verse Seven: Exchange of Self with Others

*In short, I will offer directly and indirectly*
*Every benefit and happiness to all beings, my mothers.*
*I will practice in secret taking upon myself*
*All their harmful actions and sufferings.*

The second line refers to offering every benefit to "all beings, my mothers." We must remember to offer every benefit and happiness to all of our previous mothers and not to just a few. We are not talking only about our mothers in this life, but also those from past lives. The text also says, "I will practice in secret taking upon myself all their harmful actions and suffering." We are also asking for help from the gurus, so we will be able to do this. The verse refers to the entire community of sentient beings, and all the unsought pain, illness and suffering they experience.

This seventh verse directly refers to the actual practice of tonglen. During our meditation, we accept from sentient beings all their hurts, pains, evil circumstances, interferences, illnesses, and so on. We visualize removing these hindrances from sentient beings in the form of a charcoal-colored light, and we take them upon ourselves. As it says in the *Lama Chöpa*, we are advised to mount all those things on the breath and take them into ourselves, i.e., visualize inhaling them. Whereas, when we exhale, we are to visualize sending forth all of our happiness, virtue, prosperity, comfort, great insights, and understandings. We send out all of these things and offer them to the entire community of sentient beings without discrimination. (For a more detailed explanation of how to engage in tonglen meditation, please refer to the Appendices).

### Verse Eight: Seeing All Things as Illusion

*Without these practices being defiled by the stains of the
    eight worldly concerns,
By perceiving all phenomena as illusory,
I will practice without grasping to release all beings
From the bondage of the disturbing, un-subdued mind and karma*

The eight worldly dharmas or concerns are 1) to become elated when we are praised; 2) to become unhappy when we are insulted; 3) to become happy if we receive any gifts; 4) to become unhappy if we don't; 5) to become happy upon achieving fame or success; 6) to become unhappy when we are unsuccessful; 7) to be happy when we are comfortable; and 8) to become unhappy when we are uncomfortable. The basic advice is to treat equally that which pleases us and that which displeases us. For instance, we should try to treat both a compliment and an insult as mere sound, and remain unaffected when we receive some kind of gift or when we don't. We should remain steadfast in our practice of the *Eight Verses on Thought Training*. We should see fame and lack of fame as equal and not be bothered by them, especially at the moment of our death.

Most of the time, comfort or discomfort is just a state of mind. Nothing exists on its own and proclaims itself as comfortable or uncomfortable. Rather, we decide what is and is not comfortable. These strong likes and dislikes exist only at a relative level. In the last two lines of the *Eight Verses on Thought Training*, Geshe Langri Tangpa expresses the wish that through the mind, which understands that all things are like illusions or magician's tricks, we may be freed from all clinging and attachments. This advice is not only to be used in thought training, but is to be applied to every single practice in our life. Even when reciting a single mantra such as *om mani padme hum*, we should apply it. We should also make sure our practice is not defiled by the eight worldly concerns or dharmas.

# Questions and Answers

Q. The hell realm, the hungry ghost realm, and the god realm are all unknown locations to me, and for me to understand what you're talking about, I need to know some more things to help me visualize them. I have no idea if these realms exist on the earth, and if they do exist, why can't I see them?

A. I think I understand when you say you can't visualize these places. According to the *Abhidharmakosha* text, these realms are particular places with exact locations. Of course, in the real sense, they are all an illusion. It is more or less a karmic vision that is seen by an individual. To that person, hell is an experience due to that person's individual karma. The same is also true of the hungry ghost realm. With the animal kingdom, we have no problem; we see animals everywhere.

The specific disciples for whom the *Abhidharmakosha* was written were students whose mental ability to comprehend this matter was not that good. These texts were written in accordance with their particular aptitude, predisposition, and mental capacity. When these hells are mentioned in Shantideva's *Bodhicaryavatara*, questions such as, "Who created the glowing iron surface of hell? Who created those hell sentries?" and so on are clearly answered. All these are the creation of our own negative minds. They are the clear appearance of our negative mind in a tangible form. That is very clearly stated in that text. And it was also very clearly stated by Shakyamuni Buddha.

The largest animal population is not within our sight on this earth. Most animals are very far away, in remote places beneath the ocean. But the hungry ghosts are everywhere. They do not have a specified location. They can be in the human world or anywhere else. In some texts, they do mention very specifically the eighteen main cities of the hungry ghosts. The demigods and celestial gods are also obscure to us, just like the hell beings and the hungry ghosts. We need to understand these things and to confirm them in our own mind through our studies and skilful investigation.

Q. You were talking about the verse in *Lama Chöpa* where we wish to take on the suffering of others. When I say that verse, and I really think about its meaning, I get this resistance which says, "I don't think I really mean this, and I don't think I'm ready to do this." So it's difficult to try and do that verse because I feel like I'm telling a lie.

A. If we have difficulty or extreme fear when we do these kinds of meditation, it means we are not capable of them right now. Instead, we can start with a minimum practice and gradually expand it. For example, we can take on our own personal future suffering in advance, starting by taking on the suffering of tomorrow today. Then we can take the suffering of the next month and then the suffering of the entire future.

I agree with you—this is not only your feeling but the feeling of so many other students. If we feel we are not ready for these kinds of things and we are scared, or we feel we are telling a lie, we do not need to worry, because all that we are asking is that, even though we are not capable of such a thing now, we might become capable of doing so in the near future. So at least we are asking for the option of accepting such things in the near future. We are asking for the prayer and the blessing that even though we are unable to accept the suffering of all the sentient beings upon ourselves at the present moment, we may be able to do so in the very near future.

Q. I have resistance against one of the eight verses, the one that states, "When I associate with others I think myself the lowest among all and hold them supreme." I don't understand the mind that we are supposed to be creating, to hold ourselves low and to think that others are supreme. I don't understand the humility that we are supposed to develop.

A. So you fear that if you accept yourself as the lowest of all, then they will all step on you? When we say, "May I accept myself as the lowest or the most humble amongst all," it does not mean we should compromise our confidence in ourselves. If we lose our confidence, that is the moment that we lose ourselves to others. When we accept ourself as the most humble being, extend our humility and accept ourself as the lowest, we gain strength; we do not lose strength. At that time, if we accept ourself as the lowest and at the same time share our confidence, there is no way they will look upon us as feeble, rather they will see the strength in us. We are actually talking about the mental attitude we need to share, without confiding it to others. If we verbally express what we are trying to do, they might indeed walk all over us. But if we share the attitude without sharing what we are sharing inside our mind, then there is no danger. Otherwise, some people really have a problem accepting respect. If we show respect for them, they just try to put it back on us. They are very sensitive; the more respect we offer, the more respect they return to us. Please, share that view mentally as an attitude in daily life, but never confide that attitude to anybody.

Q. Generally they say that you can't actually take on the suffering of other people, but under certain circumstances it is possible. What are the circumstances, conditions, or causes?

A. Your statement is correct. Under certain circumstances, these things do happen with some very competent practitioners. It did happen in Tibet with a Kadampa lama meditating on tonglen. As he was meditating on the veranda of his house, a beggar came by to ask for food. The family dog kept barking at him, so the beggar hit the dog with a stick. Immediately the lama had immense empathy for the dog. The lama's head began to swell on the same spot where the dog was hit. Of course the beggar did not hit the lama with the stick. But the lama did receive a bruise on his head. Just where the dog was hurt, the lama was hurt also. But when the bruise appeared on the head of the lama, it was not because the dog's karma ripened in the lama, but because in a previous life the dog and lama had somehow hit that man. Maturation occurred mutually in both the lama and the dog.

There were other instances during the life of the Buddha. There was a war between the Shakya clan and the king of Kosala, and many of the Shakyas were killed by the king's army. Then Ananda requested the Buddha to do something to stop the killing of the Shakya people. Buddha's answer was that the karmas that have not yet matured can be corrected, but the karmas that are already in the fruition period cannot; even buddhas cannot alter that. To prove that, Buddha miraculously brought before him two young men of the Shakya clan and kept them close to him. When the battle was finished and all the Shakya tribe were killed, the two youths that Buddha had with him were also dead. Of course there was no battle happening near the Buddha. No finger was ever lifted against them. But somehow they also died together with their clan. Some karma that has been collected together reaches fruition at the same time. Karma maturation is beyond fathoming; it cannot be understood easily.

So, what we really need to learn to develop is a strong firsthand conviction of the infallibility of the law of cause and effect. In addition to that, we should try to develop as much renunciation and bodhicitta as we can and attain as much understanding of emptiness as possible.

# ▪ PART THREE: *The Thirty-Seven Bodhisattva Practices*

The Root Verses

The Commentary on the Root Verses

Questions & Answers

*Togmey Zangpo*

# The Root Verses

## Supplication

*I pay heartfelt homage to you, Lokeshvara;*
*You have true compassion extending to all.*

*To those who in all of the comings and goings*
*Have seen that all things are inherently void,*
*And thus can devote both their time and their efforts*
*With one aim in mind "Let me benefit all!"*
*To such foremost Gurus and you, Lokeshvara,*
*All-seeing protector, with utmost respect,*
*I bow down before you in constant obeisance,*
*And turn to your service my thoughts, words and deeds.*

## Author's Pledge

*The fully enlightened Victorious Buddhas,*
*From whom all true pleasure and benefits come,*
*Have reached their attainment by following Dharma*
*And leading their lives through this highest of paths.*
*To live by the Dharma depends on full knowledge*
*Of how we must practice and what we must do,*
*And so I'll attempt here a brief explanation*
*Of what is the practice of all Bodhisattvas.*

*(1) This sound human body endowed with full leisure -*
*An excellent vessel rare to be found*
*Since now we've obtained one in no way deficient,*
*Let's work night and day without veering off course*
*To take 'cross the ocean and free from samsara*
*Not only ourselves but all others as well.*
*First listen, think hard, then do much meditation -*
*The Bodhisattvas all practice this way.*

*(2) Remaining too long in one place our attraction*
*To loved ones upsets us, we're tossed in its wake.*
*The flames of our anger toward those who annoy us*
*Consume what good merit we've gained in the past.*
*The darkness of closed-minded thought dims our outlook,*
*We lose vivid sight of what's right and what's wrong.*
*We must give up our home and set forth from our country -*
*The Bodhisattvas all practice this way.*

*(3) Withdrawing ourselves from the things that excite us,*
*Our mental disturbances slowly decline.*
*Ridding our minds of directionless wandering,*
*Attention on virtue will surely increase.*
*As wisdom gets clearer, the world comes in focus,*
*Our confidence grows in the Dharma we've learned.*
*We must live by ourselves far away in seclusion*
*The Bodhisattvas all practice this way.*

*(4) No matter how long we've been living together,*
*Good friends and relations must some day depart.*
*Our wealth and possessions collected with effort*
*Are left far behind at the end of our lives.*

Our mind's but a guest in our body's great guest house,
One day it must vacate and travel beyond.
We must cast away thoughts just concerning this lifetime -
The Bodhisattvas all practice this way.

(5) From staying together with friends who misguide us,
Our hatred, desires, and ignorance grow.
We're left little time to continue our studies;
We don't think of Dharma; we meditate less.
Our love and compassion for all sentient beings
Are lost and forgotten while under their sway.
We must sever our ties with misleading companions -
The Bodhisattvas all practice this way.

(6) Entrusting ourselves to the hands of a Guru
And completely relying for guidance on him,
Our competence both in the scriptures and practice
Will expand like the moon growing full and complete.
We'll solve all our problems, dispel our delusions,
By placing our confidence in him with trust.
We must cherish our Guru far more than our body -
The Bodhisattvas all practice this way.

(7) The gods of this world are not free yet from sorrow,
They're caught in samsara, some time they must fall.
If they're bound as we are, how can they protect us?
How can someone in prison free anyone else?
But Buddha, his teachings and those who live by them
Are free to give comfort - they'll not let us down.
We must go to the Three Jewels of Refuge for shelter -
The Bodhisattvas all practice this way.

*(8) The Buddha has said that the grief past endurance*
*Of creatures whose lives contain nothing but pain*
*Is misfortunate fruit of the wrongs they've committed*
*Against other beings in lifetimes gone by.*
*Not wishing to suffer from horrible torment,*
*Not flinching if even our lives are at stake,*
*We must turn from all actions that harm other beings -*
*The Bodhisattvas all practice this way.*

*(9) Like the dew that remains for a moment or two*
*On the tips of the grass and then melts with the dawn,*
*The pleasures we find in the course of our lifetimes*
*Last only an instant, they cannot endure;*
*While the freedom we gain when becoming a Buddha*
*Is a blissful attainment not subject to change.*
*We must aim all our efforts to this high achievement -*
*The Bodhisattvas all practice this way.*

*(10) In all of our lifetimes, in each incarnation,*
*We've been cared for by others with motherly love.*
*While these mothers of ours are still lost in samsara,*
*How cruel to ignore them and free just ourselves!*
*To save other beings, though countless in number,*
*To free from their sorrows these mothers of ours,*
*Produce Bodhichitta, the wish to be Buddha -*
*The Bodhisattvas all practice this way.*

*(11) All of our sufferings, without an exception,*
*Derive from the wish to please only ourselves;*
*While the thoughts and the actions that benefit others*
*Conceive and give birth to supreme Buddhahood.*

*And so, in exchange for our selfish desires*
*And shameful neglect of our suffering kin,*
*Replace thoughts of self with concern for all others -*
*The Bodhisattvas all practice this way.*

*(12) If under the sway of compulsive desire*
*And longing for things that he does not possess,*
*Some misfortunate person has stolen our riches*
*Or lets others steal them while he just stands by;*
*Then out of compassion and with no attachment,*
*To him we must dedicate all of our prayers,*
*May he have wealth and our body and merits -*
*The Bodhisattvas all practice this way.*

*(13) Although we're not guilty of any offenses*
*And never have harmed anyone in our lives,*
*If someone deluded should threaten to kill us*
*Because he is crazed with a tormented mind,*
*Then mercifully wishing for him not to suffer*
*From further misfortune because of his state,*
*We must take on ourselves the effects of his actions -*
*The Bodhisattvas all practice this way.*

*(14) If someone insulting should spread ugly rumors*
*About us with cruel words unpleasant to hear,*
*And even if what he has said spreads to others*
*And gains wide acceptance as being the truth;*
*Yet out of our wish for the one who's maligned us*
*To conquer his troubles and gain peace of mind,*
*We must practice all virtues and treat him with kindness -*
*The Bodhisattvas all practice this way.*

*(15) If we're in the midst of a large crowd of people*
*And someone should single us out for abuse,*
*Exposing our faults before all within hearing*
*And pointing out clearly the flaws we still have;*
*Then not getting angry nor being defensive,*
*Just listening in silence and heeding his words,*
*We must bow in respect to this man as our teacher -*
*The Bodhisattvas all practice this way.*

*(16) If someone we love and have cared for with kindness,*
*As an unselfish mother would cherish her child,*
*Should shun our devotion with thankless resentment*
*And treat us as if we're his most hated foe,*
*Then seeing these acts as a terrible sickness*
*Befallen our child and affecting his mind,*
*We must treat him with even more love and affection -*
*The Bodhisattvas all practice this way.*

*(17) If by our own equals or those who are lower*
*In intellect, spiritual level, or wealth,*
*We're insulted and treated as if we were nothing*
*By the force of their pride and their jealous contempt,*
*Then seeing that they are like Gurus to teach us*
*To be always humble and conquer our pride,*
*We must treat them with honor and place them above us -*
*The Bodhisattvas all practice this way.*

*(18) If we are but men of most meager subsistence*
*And always receive a great deal of abuse,*
*If we find ourselves constantly gripped by much sickness*
*And experience harm, interruption and pain,*

*Then accepting ourselves all these hardships that others*
*Would have to have suffered from wrongs they had done,*
*We must never lose courage to take pain from others -*
*The Bodhisattvas all practice this way.*

*(19) Though praised and well-known and admired by many*
*Who act most respectful by bowing their heads,*
*Though having obtained a vast treasure of riches,*
*Which equals the store of the great God of Wealth,*
*Yet seeing full well that this fruit of samsara,*
*Though fortunate, still has no essence at all,*
*We must cast out what pride we might have in these glories -*
*The Bodhisattvas all practice this way.*

*(20) If anger that dwells in our hearts lies neglected*
*And turning instead to our external foes,*
*We try to destroy them and even kill thousands,*
*Then thousands of others will plague us still more.*
*So seeing this action is not a solution,*
*Let's muster the forces of mercy and love;*
*Turn inwards and tame the wild flow of our mind-stream -*
*The Bodhisattvas all practice this way.*

*(21) Indulging in objects our senses run after*
*And drinking salt water are one and the same:*
*The more we partake, for our own satisfaction,*
*The more our desires and thirst for them grow.*
*Thus when we conceive a compulsive attraction*
*Toward whatever object our senses desire,*
*Abandon it quickly without hesitation -*
*The Bodhisattvas all practice this way.*

*(22) Whatever appears to be truly existent*
*Is just what our mind in delusion creates;*
*This mind of ours also is, from the beginning,*
*Devoid of an essence inherently real.*
*Then seeing that Truth is beyond the conceptions*
*We have of the known and the knower as well,*
*Dispel the belief in inherent existence -*
*The Bodhisattvas all practice this way.*

*(23) Whenever we meet with a beautiful object,*
*Or something attractive that pleases our mind,*
*Then do not be fooled into thinking it differs*
*In fact from a summertime rainbow:*
*Though both of them have such a lovely appearance,*
*There's nothing substantial behind this facade.*
*Abandon the drives of compulsive attraction -*
*The Bodhisattvas all practice this way.*

*(24) The various ills in our life that we suffer*
*Resemble the death of our child in a dream;*
*To hold as the truth what is merely illusion*
*Is needless exhaustion of body and mind.*
*For this very reason, when faced with unpleasant*
*Conditions that normally cause us much grief,*
*Approach them as if they were only illusion -*
*The Bodhisattvas all practice this way.*

*(25) The beings who strive to be fully enlightened*
*Would give up their bodies pursuing this aim;*
*With this high example, what need is the mention*
*Of gifts we should make of the objects we have.*

*Without any hopes of return for our kindness,*
*Or thinking about all the merit we gain,*
*Engage in the practice of generous giving -*
*The Bodhisattvas all practice this way.*

*(26) If lacking strict moral control of our conduct*
*We haven't been able to reach our own goals,*
*How can we fulfill all the wishes of others?*
*Undisciplined effort is surely absurd!*
*We have to renounce first attachment to pleasures*
*Which binds us so tightly to samsara's wheel,*
*Then protect all our vows of sworn moral behavior -*
*The Bodhisattvas all practice this way.*

*(27) For all Bodhisattvas with minds set on merit*
*Who wish to amass a great store of good deeds,*
*Encounters with those causing harm and destruction*
*Which test their commitment are mines of great wealth.*
*For this very reason, abandon resentment*
*And anger directed toward those who do harm;*
*Perfect meditation on patient endurance -*
*The Bodhisattvas all practice this way.*

*(28) If Shravakas as well as Pratyekabuddhas,*
*Who work toward Nirvana for only themselves,*
*Exert so much effort fulfilling their purpose*
*That were they in flames they'd not budge from their goal,*
*Then how much more energy must be expended*
*By those of us working for everyone's sake;*
*Enlightenment calls for the most perseverance -*
*The Bodhisattvas all practice this way.*

(29) *Higher insight that penetrates right to the essence,*
*Revealing the true way in which things exist,*
*Can only root out our emotional problems*
*If mental quiescence is laid as its base.*
*So exceeding the four formless states of absorption*
*We must work to achieve single-minded control*
*And the full concentration of deep meditation -*
*The Bodhisattvas all practice this way.*

(30) *Perfection of charity, patience, and morals,*
*Absorption and effort just isn't enough;*
*Without the Perfection of Wisdom these five are*
*Unable to bring us to full Buddhahood.*
*With the methods of pure Bodhichitta develop*
*The wisdom to see that the actor, the act,*
*And the acted upon lack inherent existence -*
*The Bodhisattvas all practice this way.*

(31) *Without making efforts to analyze clearly*
*Delusions we have and mistakes we commit,*
*Then even though outwardly practicing Dharma,*
*We still may perform many non-Dharma deeds.*
*For this very reason, let's try to examine*
*Mistakes and delusions and faults we possess,*
*And afterwards try to remove them completely -*
*The Bodhisattvas all practice this way.*

(32) *While speaking of others, the force of delusion*
*May cause us to talk of the flaws they possess;*
*If those we find fault in should be Bodhisattvas,*
*Our own reputation will suffer instead.*

*So don't run the risk of disparaging others*
*Who've entered upon Mahayana's great path;*
*Only the faults that we have should we mention -*
*The Bodhisattvas all practice this way.*

*(33) Domestic disputes with our friends and relations,*
*To gain their respect or the things we feel due,*
*Will leave us unable to listen to Dharma,*
*Unable to study or meditate well.*
*Since danger is found in the homes of our patrons,*
*As well as in those of our family and friends,*
*Abandon attachment we have to these households -*
*The Bodhisattvas all practice this way.*

*(34) The words of abuse that we utter in anger*
*Cause others much pain by disturbing their minds;*
*And we who are striving to be Bodhisattvas*
*Will find that our practice will surely decline.*
*So seeing the faults that arise from harsh language,*
*Which those who must hear find unpleasant to bear,*
*Abandon abuse that's directed toward others -*
*The Bodhisattvas all practice this way.*

*(35) Defiled types of actions will soon become habits*
*As we grow accustomed to base states of mind;*
*A great deal of effort will then be required*
*For the force of opponents to counter these stains.*
*So armed with the weapons alertness and memory,*
*Attack such defilements as lust on first sight;*
*Remove these obstructions that hinder our progress -*
*The Bodhisattvas all practice this way.*

*(36) In short, then, whatever we do in whatever*
*Condition or circumstance we might confront*
*Should be done with the force of complete self-awareness,*
*Which comprehends fully the state of our mind.*
*Then always possessing alertness and memory,*
*Which keep us in focus and ready to serve,*
*We must work for the welfare of all sentient beings -*
*The Bodhisattvas all practice this way.*

*(37) All merits we gain from the efforts we're making*
*To put into practice these virtuous ways,*
*Which we do for the sake of removing the suffering*
*Endured by the limitless mothers we've had,*
*We must dedicate purely for them to be Buddhas,*
*With wisdom that sees that both they and ourselves*
*As well as this merit all lack true existence -*
*The Bodhisattvas all practice this way.*

*By carefully following all of the teachings*
*My most holy Gurus have given to me*
*Concerning the meanings of sutra and tantra*
*Explained by the Buddhas and masters of old,*
*I've written this work on the practices numbering*
*Thirty and seven of all Buddhas' Children*
*To benefit those who desire to follow*
*The path that all Bodhisattvas must tread.*

*Because of my poor intellectual powers*
*And meager amount of the training I've had,*
*I haven't been able to write polished verses*
*In meter and style that would please those with skill;*

*But as I've relied on the words of the sutras*
*And all that my most holy Gurus have taught,*
*I'm certain that this is without any errors;*
*This truly is what Buddhas' Children have all done.*

*However, because the extent and the depth*
*Of the great waves of conduct of all Buddhas' Children*
*Are hard to be fathomed by someone of limited*
*Powers of intellect as is myself,*
*There're bound to be faults, contradictions in meaning,*
*Disjointed connections and many such flaws;*
*So most holy Gurus, I beg your indulgence,*
*Be patient with all the shortcomings I have.*

*With pure Bodhichitta of ultimate voidness,*
*Yet relative nature of mercy and love,*
*Devoid of extremes of this worldly existence*
*And passive absorption in blissful release,*
*May all sentient beings receiving the merit*
*Amassed by the effort I've made in this work*
*Soon reach your attainment, great Lokeshvara,*
*All-seeing protector with love for us all.*

This work, called *Thirty-seven Practices of All Buddhas' Children* has been composed by the bodhisattva Togmey Zangpo (1245-1369 CE), a teacher of scripture and logic, in a cave near the town of Ngulchü-rinchen in Tibet, for both his own benefit and for the sake of all others.

*Lama Tsongkhapa*

# The Commentary on the Root Verses

## HISTORICAL BACKGROUND

WITH THE PREVIOUS DHARMA TEACHINGS as a foundation, I can now begin to explain the *Thirty-Seven Bodhisattva Practices*. The word for practice in the title is *lag-len*. *Lag* means hand, and *len* means to handle. So, these are thirty-seven things which are handled by the bodhisattva. It does not mean something is handled as a tangible thing; here it means handled as a practice. These thirty-seven verses divide the bodhisattva path into the thirty-seven major practices of a bodhisattva.

This text was composed by the bodhisattva Togmey Zangpo. The English translation of the author's name is unhindered goodness: *Togmey* means unhindered and *Zangpo* means goodness. He was a Sakya scholar who lived over 600 years ago, and he embodied the qualities that this text sets forth.

## BECOMING A BODHISATTVA

At the moment we become a bodhisattva, all the buddhas of the three times prostrate to us. At that moment we have become the most courageous being, because we have accepted the responsibility of working for the welfare of all sentient beings, without any favoritism on the basis of closeness or distance. Since we have accepted this responsibility and have become the most courageous being, all the buddhas of the three times bow and make prostration to us. Thus, the Buddha addressed the bodhisattva Kashyapa, saying, "Oh, Kashyapa, those who have strong faith in me should not make prostrations to the tathagatas [buddhas], but to the bodhisattvas."

It is for that reason that we adopt becoming a bodhisattva as our personal goal. Even though we may not be able to achieve that goal in this life, we should at least try to keep that goal in mind. Whatever the active duties of a bodhisattva are, we need to emulate those duties in our daily life. If we do that, then whatever we do becomes most productive and effective. The goal is to work absolutely for the wellbeing of the entire community of sentient beings. The moment one becomes a bodhisattva, one's utmost responsibility is working for the welfare of all sentient beings. This is the key work of the bodhisattvas. The reason is that, at that moment, the bodhisattva is totally under the influence of a properly trained mind which cherishes all sentient beings. He or she has totally overcome the self-cherishing mind, so that self-cherishing thoughts no longer arise even in dreams.

Because of these reasons, the bodhisattvas are often addressed as the Buddha's children. All the activities of their daily lives can be called activities of the Buddha's children. Entering into the activities of the bodhisattvas by consistent engagement, we achieve the most meaningful state—final buddhahood. At that moment, we have achieved the maximum benefit that we can attain in this human rebirth.

Here, the topic to be discussed is the *Thirty-Seven Bodhisattva Practices*, which may be described as the thirty-seven deeds of the bodhisattvas, or the thirty-seven essential job descriptions of the bodhisattvas. Once we become bodhisattvas, these duties become very important; we cannot be a bodhisattva without them. We all share the same thought: our strong wish is to be a bodhisattva, our strong prayer is that some day we may become a bodhisattva, and our strong desire is that we may be able to act like a bodhisattva. Since we share these three things—we wish, we pray, and we try to emulate their example—it becomes very important for us to understand the various duties and deeds of bodhisattvas, so that we engage in them correctly.

## THE COMMENTARY

## Supplication

*Namo Lokeshvara*

*I pay heartfelt homage to you, Lokeshvara;*
*You have true compassion extending to all.*

*To those who in all of the comings and goings*
*Have seen that all things are inherently void,*
*And thus can devote both their time and their efforts*
*With one aim in mind "Let me benefit all!"*
*To such foremost Gurus and you, Lokeshvara,*
*All-seeing protector, with utmost respect,*
*I bow down before you in constant obeisance,*
*And turn to your service my thoughts, words and deeds.*

We can roughly organize all the activities of the bodhisattvas in a brief form of thirty-seven practices. In the beginning of every text you will see a supplication. Then there will be a pledge by the writer to complete his work. There are two reasons why a writer makes a supplication at the beginning of a text: first, in order to be able to complete the work without any major obstacles and, second, to achieve the ultimate benefit, liberation. As supplication, the author says *Namo Lokeshvara*, which means, "I bow down to Avalokiteshvara (Tib: Chenrezig)." The supplication starts with the Tibetan word *gang*, which here refers to Avalokiteshvara who has compassion although he sees all dharmas, or things, as neither coming nor going. Of course, conventionally things

have movement; they come and go, don't they? But the author is referring to those beings who see everything as devoid of inherent coming
or going. In essence, this means that things do not come and go by
themselves. Although you, Avalokiteshvara, see all things as inherently devoid of coming or going, you are dedicated solely to the welfare of sentient beings. Avalokiteshvara, the one who performs these
deeds, to you with all my three doors—body, speech, and mind—I
make my prostrations.

### Author's Pledge

*The fully enlightened Victorious Buddhas,*
*From whom all true pleasure and benefits come,*
*Have reached their attainment by following Dharma*
*And leading their lives through this highest of paths.*
*To live by the Dharma depends on full knowledge*
*Of how we must practice and what we must do,*
*And so I'll attempt here a brief explanation*
*Of what is the practice of all Bodhisattvas.*

All the buddhas, it says, are the result of the practice of the holy
dharma. Since we need to know how to practice, and since we depend
on skill in practice, the author, Togmey Zangpo, writes about how to
carry out the practices of the bodhisattvas or the Buddha's children.
He promises to write about how to put the work of bodhisattvas into
practice. There are two reasons why he makes this promise: 1) that
promise helps the author to complete the work, and 2) his acts emulate the works of the holy beings.

We find the same thing in other great works such as Maitreya's *Abhisamayalamkara*. In the beginning, you will see the author's supplication
and his promise concerning what he is to write. Whatever promise or
pledges they make, it is like something that is inscribed in stone—

unchangeable and unwavering. This promise helps the authors to complete their work, whereas our promises are like an inscription on water.

### Verse One: Enthusiastic Perseverance

*This sound human body endowed with full leisure -*
*An excellent vessel rare to be found*
*Since now we've obtained one in no way deficient,*
*Let's work night and day without veering off course*
*To take 'cross the ocean and free from samsara*
*Not only ourselves but all others as well.*
*First listen, think hard, then do much meditation—*
*The Bodhisattvas all practice this way.*

After the supplication and the author's promise comes the beginning of the actual verses. As practitioners, we need both the freedoms and the endowments of a precious human rebirth, because without them, our practice becomes impossible. The hell beings do not have these qualities; nor do the hungry ghosts or most of the animals. First of all, they do not have freedom or any spare moments for practice; second, even if they did have time for practice, they do not have the endowments, or faculties, with which to practice. There are some human worlds as well as some celestial worlds that do have the endowments or faculties, but they do not have the freedom or time for practice. Likewise, some human worlds have the freedom, but lack the endowments. This is very important. This perfect human rebirth, one complete with all the freedoms and endowments, is extremely rare. We have received such an opportunity, which is so very difficult to find!

So the verse says, at this opportunity or at this moment, in order to deliver oneself as well as all others from this great ocean of samsara, without discriminating whether it is day or night, we need to engage all the time in the three wisdoms: learning, reflection, and meditation on the teachings. Engaging oneself in learning, reflection, and enthusiastic meditation on the teachings all the time is one of the bodhisattva practices. Enthusiastic perseverance enables us to engage in the thirty-seven thoughts and meditations on the teachings day and night. This will enable us to best utilize this opportune moment, a time in which we have received this perfect human rebirth with all its freedoms and endowments.

With enthusiastic perseverance, we are able to be either studying or thinking about the teachings, maintaining the continuity of that thought, and putting that into meditation. Doing these three different activities correctly, day and night, enhances our practice. I understand very well that it is extremely hard for us to do this practice. First of all we have to keep our job, and second, we need some recreation time, and time for other things as well. It becomes very difficult to do continuously what is required here. At least we can set aside time for one or two sessions a day. During that time we can allow ourselves to be free from all other chores and concerns and give some time to study. By study I mean reading a dharma book, trying to contemplate on its contents, and debating about what we have read. Then meditate on that. We have other practices to do, but try to set aside time for at least one session per day. So, if we do that, we can start as an initial practitioner.

### Verse Two: Abandoning the Birthplace

*Remaining too long in one place our attraction*
*To loved ones upsets us, we're tossed in its wake.*
*The flames of our anger toward those who annoy us*
*Consume what good merit we've gained in the past.*
*The darkness of closed-minded thought dims our outlook,*
*We lose vivid sight of what's right and what's wrong.*
*We must give up our home and set forth from our country—*
*The Bodhisattvas all practice this way.*

The second bodhisattva practice is to abandon our birthplace. I do not see this as a problem for any of us because many of us were born somewhere else. But the reason the author said we need to abandon our birthplace is not for the sake of abandonment itself. No, the reason is that if we live in one place for a long time we build up a very strong attachment, or clinging, to that place as well as to certain groups of people, such as our relatives or friends. Also, we develop strong aversion towards certain groups of people who are labeled as adversaries and so forth. To avoid such things, the author encourages us to abandon them. It says that our attachments to our relatives or friends are just like the waves are to the ocean; they are that closely associated with the person, whereas the strong belief in hatred when we see our adversary is like a burning flame. Under such circumstances, we become totally ignorant of what we are expected to do and what we are expected not to do. We are busy taking care of relatives and getting rid of enemies. When we are completely blind to such a distinction, that is the moment we need to abandon that place and move.

What the text emphasizes here is the need for development of equanimity toward everybody. The author encourages us to do three things: 1) reduce the strong wave or surge of attachments; 2) reduce the heat of the blaze of hatred; and 3) lessen the thickness or darkness of ignorance that is caused by these things. In other texts, they say a birthplace is like a dungeon or a prison, and our relatives and friends are like prison guards. The reason is that when we cling to them very strongly and we are deeply attached to them, that makes us more solidly grounded in the depths of samsara. The second practice says to give up our birthplace, but we are not to read that as just the birthplace. What we are trying to get rid of here, as the author clearly mentions, are attachment, hatred, and ignorance. Those are the things that we are trying to reduce or eliminate.

### Verse Three: Being Free from Distractions

*Withdrawing ourselves from the things that excite us,*
*Our mental disturbances slowly decline.*
*Ridding our minds of directionless wandering,*
*Attention on virtue will surely increase.*
*As wisdom gets clearer, the world comes in focus,*
*Our confidence grows in the Dharma we've learned.*
*We must live by ourselves far away in seclusion—*
*The Bodhisattvas all practice this way.*

The next step is to be free from distractions. If we are free from distractions, then virtuous practice automatically becomes successful. For that reason, let's talk about distraction. Disturbance or distraction is counter to *samadhi* or mental concentration; it opposes concentration or mental stability. Distraction diverts us from our intended focus and brings us one thought after another. Thus we postpone what we originally intended to do. For instance, what causes us to miss our commitment to say a prayer? What causes us to transgress the vows that we once promised to keep? And what causes us to take away time from some important chores we decided to do for the day? All of the situations that take us away from those important things that we must do, if we check, are all caused by distractions. Therefore, it is imperative that we abandon such distractions.

The text says to give up our birthplace, and also to give up distractions. In addition to that, we need to have a clear mind—one that is sharp in the sense of being able to deliberate on the subject matter very clearly. Our mind should not be fuzzy. The result of this sharp mind is a strong faith and conviction in our dharma practice and subsequently, a strong certainty about what we are doing. In order to develop this sharp mind, solitude is important.

For these reasons, seeking solitude becomes one of the practices of the bodhisattva. The solution is to seek solitude, but seeking solitude does not mean going into an isolated area or isolating ourselves from everybody. If that were the only requirement, then certainly birds and animals that choose to live in a very secluded area must have wonderful contemplation; but that is not the case. The true purpose for seeking isolation is explained by Lama Tsongkhapa, who said that if we want to realize the essential meaning of the three principle aspects of the path—renunciation, bodhicitta, and insight into emptiness (*shunyata*)—that is the time when we should seek isolation or seclusion.

### Verse Four: Abandoning Preoccupation with this Life

*No matter how long we've been living together,*
*Good friends and relations must some day depart.*
*Our wealth and possessions collected with effort*
*Are left far behind at the end of our lives.*
*Our mind's but a guest in our body's great guest house,*
*One day it must vacate and travel beyond.*
*We must cast away thoughts just concerning this lifetime—*
*The Bodhisattvas all practice this way.*

This verse says that giving up the preoccupation with our welfare in this life is one of the practices of the bodhisattvas. Can we really do this? The author says that we can and explains first why we should and how we can do it. Giving up preoccupation with this life does not mean to go ahead and commit suicide, but rather to give up major concerns about food, clothes, and fame; we should not be too attached to those things. The author is encouraging us to have no attachments to those things, but he does not tell us to starve ourselves. As long as we are unable to sever our attachments to food, clothes, and fame, any dharma practice we may be doing is not an authentic or true dharma practice because of the motivation. So there is a fine line between dharma and non-dharma activities. Any activity that is done for the wellbeing of the life after this life or for future lives becomes a dharma deed, whereas anything done only out of concern for this life becomes a non-dharma activity. That is the reason we need to give up our preoccupation with our welfare in this life alone.

Are we able to do that? Can we do that? The answer is yes. Certainly we can give up preoccupation with this life. Just think, those with whom we have lived for many years, or those whom we have accompanied for many years, such as our parents, relatives and siblings, will all leave one day. Whenever death and impermanence strike us, we cannot ask for a delay. We cannot say, "Could I be spared for a few moments because I have not seen my parents and relatives for so long, I have more chores to complete, or I would like to finish something that remains to be done." Whenever death comes, we cannot talk it into leaving us for even an extra moment. At that moment of separation, any number of relatives we may have, or any amount of wealth we have acquired, or any celebrated status we have gained in our lives cannot help. The product of our lifelong effort and hard work is left behind when we face death. In a similar manner, this very precious body, which is very dear to us and which has served us as a guest house from birth until now, is also left behind. We become like guests checking out of a guest house. Our mind is singled out, and it leaves on its own.

I think this section belongs to what we refer to as lam-rim, and it also belongs under the section of impermanence and death. If we could think over these things every single day, that would be very helpful. From among these three concerns—food, clothes, and fame—it is easier to give up a little or withstand some loss of our food and clothes, but it is really difficult to give up fame. However, we must not cling to fame or notoriety, because no matter how famous we become in our lifetime, at the moment of death the world is left behind us. As a person, we cannot take it along with us. We may acquire a symbol of our celebrated status or fame in the form of an inscription on stone, but that stone inscription which serves as a memorial for us does not help us a bit as one who is departing. It is almost like being a beggar who has just acquired the name of a king but still remains poor and starving. The name provides no real benefit.

### Verse Five: Avoiding Evil Friends

*From staying together with friends who misguide us,*
*Our hatred, desires, and ignorance grow.*
*We're left little time to continue our studies;*
*We don't think of Dharma; we meditate less.*
*Our love and compassion for all sentient beings*
*Are lost and forgotten while under their sway.*
*We must sever our ties with misleading companions—*
*The Bodhisattvas all practice this way.*

The fifth verse says that staying away from evil friends is a practice of the bodhisattvas. Actually, the need to stay away from evil friends, even though it says it is one of the bodhisattva practices, is meant for us as beginning practitioners. For bodhisattvas, who are quite advanced, this is hardly a problem; but for us aspirants to bodhisattvahood or for those of us who are taking a couple of steps toward becoming a bodhisattva, for such a very fragile practitioner, this is important. What do we lose if we keep the company of evil friends? What kind of behavior do we acquire? Do these evil friends appear like the devil with long horns on their heads or long hair on their bodies? Not necessarily. An evil friend is anybody who causes a rift between us and our virtuous practices, and who makes us more inclined towards more negative activities than before. They probably come in a very supportive form. They invite us to parties and encourage us to drink, and so on. So, it is hard to give them up, but we have to make the effort.

If we keep the company of such friends, our three poisonous negative mental states, namely attachment, hatred, and ignorance, grow. For instance, if we note that we already have a problem with attachment prior to our friendship, and if this friendship has very strong desire or very strong attachment, then we soon will be carried away by a huge wave of attachment. Also, if we already have a problem with hatred and then keep the company of an angry person, gradually his anger will rub off on us and soon that little ember of anger will turn into a huge blaze within us. For these reasons, it is very important for us, as beginners, to stay away from bad friendships. The little knowledge we have prior to such friendships, about what we ought to do and what we ought not to do, will fade away and the darkness of ignorance will cover us over. We forget the knowledge we already have, and we cease to learn anything new. Because of that, our whole mind will turn into a huge cloud of darkness. Although we may have compassion or love for other sentient beings, the influence of their friendship could cause us to lose these qualities. So these are all the reasons we need to stay away from the company of devilish friends.

### Verse Six: Treasuring the Spiritual Friend

*Entrusting ourselves to the hands of a Guru*
*And completely relying for guidance on him,*
*Our competence both in the scriptures and practice*
*Will expand like the moon growing full and complete.*
*We'll solve all our problems, dispel our delusions,*
*By placing our confidence in him with trust.*
*We must cherish our Guru far more than our body—*
*The Bodhisattvas all practice this way.*

The next step is how to treasure a spiritual master or friend. The text says to place our full confidence solely in him or her. Cherishing our guru far more than our body is one of the bodhisattva practices.

According to the lam-rim, the proper cultivation of the guru or spiritual master is the very root or foundation of all spiritual development. So the sixth verse discusses the cultivation of the spiritual master being the real root of the spiritual path. Hypothetically, somebody might ask, "If you are seriously cultivating a spiritual master, even at the cost or the risk of your own life, what benefit do you get out of doing so?" The result is that through the proper cultivation of our spiritual master, all the faults that a person could have, gradually become exhausted. All instructions provided by the spiritual master are to help us reduce those kinds of wrongdoings and wrong actions, and to enable us to overcome all negative mental states and all actions that are precipitated by those negative mental states. So a benefit of cultivating devotion to a spiritual master is that we receive the instructions to do these things, and through following these instructions, we get a chance to reduce wrongdoings and succeed. In addition to that knowledge, our spiritual development will grow like the waxing moon.

The proper cultivation of devotion to our guru or spiritual master really is the very root of all prosperity and goodness. Once again, I recommend that you read the *Lam-rim Chenmo* on this subject: the eight benefits of cultivating guru devotion, the eight disadvantages of not cultivating guru devotion, and also how to cultivate guru devotion by thought and action. Those are described in detail in the *Lam-Rim Chenmo*, and I strongly urge that we not ignore or neglect the lam-rim. Lam-rim is not at all something to be neglected; it is very important to all of us.

The importance of the proper cultivation of devotion to the guru or spiritual master is affirmed in both Tantra and Sutra; it is emphasized in both. According to Tantra especially, no matter how skillfully we have meditated on all the instructions of Tantra, if our guru devotion—our relation with our spiritual master—has gone wrong somewhere, we will not attain the realization that we want from that practice. For all of these reasons mentioned, meticulously or conscientiously cultivating a proper guru-disciple relationship is one of the important practices of a bodhisattva.

An example used quite frequently in many texts is that of a bodhisattva named Sadaprarudita, and how he cultivated devotion for his guru even at the risk of his own body and life. This instance happened many *kalpas* or eons ago, but it was retold by the Buddha in his *Prajnaparamita Sutra*. We have no shortage of examples that we can follow: we can follow the example of Naropa and how he cultivated devotion for Tilopa, how Milarepa regarded Marpa and his dedication, and how scrupulously the great Dromtönpa considered the teachings of Atisha and cultivated devotion toward him. There are the examples of many other lamas available to us, and we should try to follow these examples. Take the example of the great Lama Tsongkhapa. He maintained a very meticulous guru-disciple relationship with all his masters, both in his thought and in his deeds. He encouraged and emphasized the importance of this relationship with all of his disciples.

### Verse Seven: Taking Refuge

*The gods of this world are not free yet from sorrow,*
*They're caught in samsara, some time they must fall.*
*If they're bound as we are, how can they protect us?*
*How can someone in prison free anyone else?*
*But Buddha, his teachings and those who live by them*
*Are free to give comfort—they'll not let us down.*
*We must go to the Three Jewels of Refuge for shelter—*
*The Bodhisattvas all practice this way.*

The seventh verse says that the taking of refuge is one of the practices of a bodhisattva. We already know how important refuge is to us, but to emphasize the importance of refuge, the author says, "We must go to the Three Jewels of refuge for shelter." This is one of the most important practices of the bodhisattvas. This is because the determining factor of whether we are Buddhists, i.e., whether we have entered into Buddhist teachings, is whether or not we have taken refuge. Taking refuge is also important because we are continuously tormented by the general suffering of cyclic existence, particularly the suffering of the three lower realms. It is our personal responsibility to gain freedom from this continuous torture of cyclic existence and we cannot do this on our own at the present moment. Since it is at present beyond our personal capability, we need to find someone to assist us.

We go in search of someone who can help us break free from these kinds of cyclic problems. Some thought the sun could do that for them; others thought the moon could do that for them; and still others resorted to some powerful spirits in this world. But those powerful worldly spirits and so on cannot provide us with what we are looking for, since they themselves are in the same situation, living in the dungeon of samsara. Since they themselves are under the bondage of cyclic existence, they cannot help unbind anybody else. We might think that if we are bound or fastened with a rope, we could try to cut loose from it with our teeth. However, in this case our teeth would not be much help, because all parts of the body are bound fast by this samsara. Since they are under the same kind of bondage as ourselves, all these worldly deities and worldly spirits cannot give us the shelter or the refuge we are seeking.

So, who do we need to seek? Is there somebody who is not fraudulent, who would not let us down? We need to take refuge in the Three Jewels who are non-deceiving and non-fraudulent. This verse says that one needs to take refuge, but it does not discuss *how* to take refuge. There are two factors which enable us to take refuge: fear of cyclic existence and faith in the Three Jewels. In order to have a strong fear of the suffering of cyclic existence, particularly in the lower realms, we really need to understand the facts of samsara. However, talking about the lower realms can be very boring. Therefore, we need to contemplate the three lower realms as if we were in that situation at this moment, as if we were going through those experiences right now. In our meditation, this is what we should try to work for. Such meditation will definitely generate great fear in our heart, and that fear is something wonderful because it serves as one of the primary causes for taking refuge. The fear itself is not a solution, but it causes us to look for the solution. Since we know that fear does not solve the problem, we then look for somebody who is capable of helping us out of samsara.

When we look around, we find that the Three Jewels are capable of helping us out of cyclic existence. Since we know that they are capable, we have faith they will do so. So the second factor that enables us to take refuge is the faith that the Three Jewels are capable of doing what we are looking for. The first factor—the strong fear of cyclic existence—leads to the second factor, the faith that the Three Jewels can provide us with freedom from samsara. When we have those two combined, the fear and the faith, we are able to take immaculate refuge.

For the details of this we can go back again to the lam-rim and study about the Buddha, the Dharma, and the Sangha: the Three Jewels. You will find a lengthy discussion about them in the *Lam-Rim Chenmo*. In both Sutra and Tantra, taking refuge plays the most important role. For instance, if we choose to become an ordained being, then taking refuge serves as the beginning; it serves as the starting point. In the same way, if we choose to take tantric vows, we cannot take tantric vows without bodhisattva vows. However, the bodhisattva vows begin with taking refuge, which serves as an initial starting point for all practice. Just like the cornerstone in a building, refuge is the foundation block of the entire structure of these practices.

Verse Eight: Refraining from Negative Deeds

*The Buddha has said that the grief past endurance*
*Of creatures whose lives contain nothing but pain*
*Is misfortunate fruit of the wrongs they've committed*
*Against other beings in lifetimes gone by.*
*Not wishing to suffer from horrible torment,*
*Not flinching if even our lives are at stake,*
*We must turn from all actions that harm other beings—*
*The Bodhisattvas all practice this way.*

The eighth verse says that refraining from negative deeds is one of the practices of a bodhisattva. This means not only refraining from negative activities, but also never committing such acts, even at the cost of one's own life. This is real bodhisattva practice. Why should we choose to risk our life rather than commit a negative action? Without knowing the reasons, it is difficult to make such a choice; so I will explain. We do not desire the suffering of hell or lower realms under any circumstances. This is not acceptable to us. Even in the human realm, under no circumstances is any form of suffering or sorrow desirable. Yet, how is it that we receive suffering in so much abundance? The answer is that suffering is the fruition of karma. For this reason, we have to stop negative activities with all the effort we can exert, even at the risk of our life. Doing this is one of the major practices of the bodhisattvas.

Consequently, it is important for us to have a little knowledge about how karma, or cause and effect, works. We may say that not every act we do during a day is a negative act. This is so. There are three different kinds of karma we can commit in a day: negative acts, virtuous acts, and neutral acts. An act that ripens in the form of a beautiful result or something appealing is what we call a virtuous deed or virtuous karma. Deeds which bring unpleasant results constitute negative karma. Deeds which bring neither pleasant nor unpleasant results are called neutral karma. These explanations come from the *Lam-Rim Chenmo* and are not specifically mentioned in this text, which only refers to karma. It is our own duty to make ourselves knowledgeable about karma and its effects through a thorough study of the lam-rim and other texts. For instance, unless we have a good understanding of karma or cause and effect, it becomes very difficult for us to have an effective meditation on receiving and giving (*tonglen*).

The teaching on *The Wheel of Sharp Weapons* refers to certain causes we have created at different times. As a result, we go through corresponding experiences or encounter certain situations in our daily living. We need to learn how to practice effectively so that we can gain some control over the types of causes or karma we are creating. Karma is discussed in so many different kinds of texts and literature. What we should do is gather all that information, incorporate it into our personal mental base, and then put it into practice in our life. Blocking or refraining from negative actions is not only the responsibility of ordained beings, or monks and nuns, but is the responsibility of all of us as individuals and as bodhisattvas.

### Verse Nine: Desiring Liberation

*Like the dew that remains for a moment or two*
*On the tips of the grass and then melts with the dawn,*
*The pleasures we find in the course of our lifetimes*
*Last only an instant, they cannot endure;*
*While the freedom we gain when becoming a Buddha*
*Is a blissful attainment not subject to change.*
*We must aim all our efforts to this high achievement—*
*The Bodhisattvas all practice this way.*

The ninth verse says that having interest in or desire for attaining nirvana is one of the practices of the bodhisattvas. When we talk about nirvana or liberation, we can distinguish two kinds of nirvana: the general nirvana and the great nirvana (the nirvana of Mahayana practitioners). Both of these nirvanas are equally good, and we can show interest in either one of them. But those of us who have already decided to be a Mahayana practitioner should learn to show a greater interest in the great nirvana. Why do we need to show interest toward the great nirvana? We all have dedicated ourselves to the Mahayana path, so we choose enlightenment as our ultimate goal for two reasons: for our own personal benefit, and for the benefit of others. Without personal enlightenment, we cannot fully benefit other beings. Personal enlightenment is a must. In order to do any good for others, we need to be totally free from the two types of obscurations: namely, the obscuration that is due to negative mental states and the obscuration that obstructs one's knowledge of all things. Without overcoming these two types of obscurations, we cannot do much good for others or ourselves.

In addition to that, all the bliss and temporary happiness we find in any of the three worlds of existence are comparable to the dewdrops we find on a blade of grass; they are ephemeral, they do not last. They dry up in a moment. We may say that in the three realms—namely, the formless realm, the form realm, and the desire realm—any bliss or happiness we find therein is very minute. It is small and, in terms of duration, it is very short-lived, like the snap of a finger. On top of that, there are also experiences which come under the guise of happiness but have essentially the nature of suffering. They change into suffering, but we fail to see them as such when they appear in the form of happiness; that is our failure. Such happiness is also very short-lived, like the dewdrop on the tip of a blade of grass, because the moment the sun comes, it is bound to disappear. All worldly happiness is like this.

What we need is the kind of happiness and bliss that is stable, dependable, durable, and long-lasting. Supreme happiness is what we need. But what is supreme happiness? Supreme happiness is the state of nirvana. That state of nirvana alone is supreme happiness. Enlightenment itself is ultimate happiness. In short, the text says that seeing the importance of the ultimate state of enlightenment and seeing the trivial nature of the temporary happiness that we experience in our daily living, which lacks any true essence, is one of the practices of the bodhisattvas. Wanting the happiness of enlightenment as our ultimate goal, for our own sake as well as for the sake of all other beings, and maintaining that aspiration day and night, is one of the bodhisattva practices. For more details on this topic, refer to the section in the *Lam-Rim Chenmo* on the general suffering of samsara and particularly on the suffering of the three lower realms.

Verse Ten: Generating Bodhicitta

*In all of our lifetimes, in each incarnation,*
*We've been cared for by others with motherly love.*
*While these mothers of ours are still lost in samsara,*
*How cruel to ignore them and free just ourselves!*
*To save other beings, though countless in number,*
*To free from their sorrows these mothers of ours,*
*Produce Bodhichitta, the wish to be Buddha—*
*The Bodhisattvas all practice this way.*

The tenth verse says that generating bodhicitta is one of the practices of the bodhisattvas. Why do we need to generate bodhicitta? We don't need bodhicitta just to attain peace and nirvana for personal reasons. For instance, those arhats of the shravaka or the pratyekabuddha paths can abide in a state of happiness, free from suffering for eons and eons. Just through single-pointed concentration on a single moment of contemplation, they overcome all suffering. But this alone is insufficient for us because we know that all sentient beings, every one of them, have served either as our father or as our mother. It becomes unacceptable to sustain ourselves in the state of full happiness or bliss for eons while not caring for all the others who are immersed in suffering. What good is that happiness when we see all those who have been our parents in the midst of suffering while we alone enjoy happiness? To give a clear illustration, how would it be if one of our relatives or parents were caught and were being tortured somewhere in the vicinity, while we were at a huge party nearby enjoying ourselves? This sounds absurd, but in actuality that is exactly what is happening.

We need to understand how everyone is bound by suffering, and, understanding these facts, make a pledge to ourselves that we will accept the responsibility to free them from that bondage. But once we make that pledge (assuming the responsibility to free everybody from that bondage of suffering), we ask, "Do I have the capability or the power to do this?" Then we realize that we do not. When we look at ourselves, we find that right now we do not have the strength or the influence to do it, but looking ahead, we can see that in a state of great enlightenment we really can help others become free from their suffering. By seeing what becomes possible with the achievement of full enlightenment, we acquire the strong aspiration that "By every means I will try my best to attain the state of great enlightenment in order to benefit all these other sentient beings." Thus, we reinforce the pledge we made earlier. Once we reach that point, we have developed bodhicitta and entered the Mahayana path.

There are two ways we can develop this bodhicitta, which are explained in the *Lam-Rim Chenmo*. The first way is taking bodhicitta vows by going through a ceremony either in the presence of our guru or in front of the buddhas symbolized on the altar, thereby ritually accepting the aspiring bodhicitta. Whenever we develop a strong aspiration to attain enlightenment in order to help all other sentient beings, we are developing aspiring bodhicitta. Whereas when we cultivate engaging bodhicitta, we not only make that wish or promise, but we vow actually to engage in the activities of the bodhisattvas. That is why, in the *Bodhicaryavatara*, Shantideva compares these two types of bodhicitta to two types of travelers. The traveler who is planning to make a journey is the state of the aspiring bodhicitta, and the other who is actually on the road is the engaging bodhicitta.

You will find all of this in the *Prajnaparamita Sutra*, and the essential meaning of that sutra is organized in the *Abhisamayalamkara* in eight chapters. All the details concerning bodhicitta are in the first chapter. However, the first chapter is divided into ten elements that represent omniscience. Within those ten, the first is bodhicitta. We are encouraged to remind ourselves every single day to reinforce this aspiration and make a promise that "I will try my best to attain enlightenment in order to help all other beings." We need to think about this several times every day. For instance, we all have an altar and every morning we either make an offering of fresh flowers, incense, or a water bowl arrangement while making the wish that "By the virtue of this offering I make here, may I attain enlightenment as soon as possible for all other sentient beings." If we make that wish, that would be very helpful. Also, we should try to remind ourselves of that particular section of the bodhisattva practice where it says that the frequent aspiration to attain enlightenment for every sentient being is one of the practices of the bodhisattva.

### Verse Eleven: Exchanging Self with Others

*All of our sufferings, without an exception,*
*Derive from the wish to please only ourselves;*
*While the thoughts and the actions that benefit others*
*Conceive and give birth to supreme Buddhahood.*
*And so, in exchange for our selfish desires*
*And shameful neglect of our suffering kin,*
*Replace thoughts of self with concern for all others—*
*The Bodhisattvas all practice this way.*

The eleventh verse says that the exchanging of self with others is the practice of the bodhisattvas. How can we do this? When we say the exchange of self with others, it does not mean a change of residence with somebody else, or the exchange of gifts with others. It says that all suffering is the result of wishing happiness for oneself alone, or self-cherishing, whereas great enlightenment is the result of the mind that wishes to benefit all sentient beings. For that reason it says, "Whatever happiness I possess, I send forth for every other being, and all the sufferings of other beings, I accept upon myself." This is stated in a slightly different way in the *Bodhicaryavatara*, where it says that all misery or suffering is the result of the self-cherishing mind, whereas all happiness is the result of the mind that cherishes others.

What we need to learn is that whenever we face suffering, we need to trace its origin, asking, "How has this come about?" Whenever we face a sudden illness, our first step is to look for a doctor or some remedy to get rid of it. We never learn to face the origin or investigate the very source of that suffering. For instance, a headache is common to almost every one of us and is accompanied by a certain amount of misery. But we have to acknowledge that the misery from the headache is the result of negative deeds. This brings us back to the law of cause and effect, or karma, because it is negative karma which brings us misery. We may ask, "Was that negative cause created by myself or by some other being?" We need to check up on that. If you think about karma and how it works, then you will know that any form of karma created by some other being cannot be experienced by you. So, most certainly, we have created some cause in our past lifetime to have that headache. Either we hit somebody with a club on the head, or else we did something like that in one of our past lives, to have a similar experience in this life. In one way or another, we certainly have created the karma which has brought us this kind of headache. As a result of that negative deed, its maturation comes upon us.

Understanding these contemplations, we need to pledge to ourselves, "From now on, I will never attempt any action which harms others." We also need to understand that all happiness is the result of virtuous deeds. The attainment of great enlightenment is the result of helping others or wishing to help others. We need to realize that without bodhicitta we cannot attain enlightenment. We know very clearly how to develop bodhicitta. Through this kind of thought process, we learn that we need to engage in the practice of exchanging oneself with others. It says in the *Lama Chöpa*, "What the buddhas have gained through the virtue of cherishing others, and what all sentient beings have gained from cherishing themselves alone; with the mind that is able to see the difference between those two, may I be able to exchange myself for others."

Since we only care for ourselves alone, we are still immersed in samsara. Whereas since the buddhas think of others exclusively, they attain enlightenment. Many eons ago, Shakyamuni Buddha and we were all in the same situation, caught up in samsara, but because the Buddha cared about others exclusively and ignored his own selfish attitude, he became what he is, that is, enlightened. From this kind of analysis, we should learn to exchange ourselves for others. You will find this topic covered in the bodhicitta section of the *Lam-Rim Chenmo*. All the information about such works as the *Ratnavali*, or *Precious Garland*, by Nagarjuna, the *Madhyamakavatara* by Chandrakırti, and the *Bodhicaryavatara* by Shantideva is gathered together in the *Lam-Rim Chenmo* and presented in a very understandable and condensed form, giving us the steps to develop the mind through the exchange of oneself with others.

Verse Twelve: Dedicating Body, Wealth, and Virtues

*If under the sway of compulsive desire*
*And longing for things that he does not possess,*
*Some misfortunate person has stolen our riches*
*Or lets others steal them while he just stands by;*
*Then out of compassion and with no attachment,*
*To him we must dedicate all of our prayers,*
*May he have wealth and our body and merits—*
*The Bodhisattvas all practice this way.*

The twelfth verse says that dedicating one's body, belongings, and personal virtue, to the welfare of others, is one of the practices of the bodhisattvas. Generally speaking, both the Sutra and the Tantra emphasize the need for dedicating our body, belongings or wealth, and our virtue to the benefit of others. Particularly, if we have received any tantric initiations and are a practicing student, then we are pledge-bound to dedicate our body, belongings, and our merit to others, six times a day. But just saying it six times a day is not sufficient. What is meant by dedicating is to give all three from the depth of our heart. So, strictly speaking, we no longer own any of these three because we have already dedicated them to others. But, if we do not own them, how are we supposed to use them? Since they are owned by others, we need to use them in order to attain the fullest enlightenment for the sake of others. It is almost like an estate that is given to the state or some organization, where we manage that estate still conducting the daily transactions by ourself, while the ownership belongs to somebody else. Similarly, even though our body, wealth, and virtue do not belong to us since we have dedicated them to all sentient beings, we still need to use them to attain enlightenment for the sake of others.

Particularly, if you have bodhisattva vows, then you need to dedicate all these resources for others every single day, six times a day.

Those who have pratimoksha vows, like nuns or monks, are not allowed to keep too many things anyway. However, if we manage some property for others' sake, then it is not a transgression of these vows. We can be the manager of the property, making it available for others whenever the need arises. In many circumstances, we have to weigh between restriction and benefit, and go by whichever seems stronger. Suppose some greedy man comes by and takes away everything we own or hires somebody to rob us. If somebody robs us like that, then instead of getting angry, we just dedicate all our merits of the three times for their sake. Being able to do this is one of the practices of the bodhisattvas. For example, if a burglar comes and takes something, then we are to give him the rest and thank him for doing so. This means that if somebody robs us, we must not show anger toward that person, but instead we should learn to dedicate our virtue and everything for that person's sake. Even though it is the hardest thing to do, learning to dedicate our merit and wealth to somebody who harms us is one of the essential practices of the bodhisattvas.

I would like to go into a little more detail on this subject. Among these three things, body, wealth and merit, the best gift we can give is the dedication of our merits. As for giving wealth, there are two types: our personal wealth and the wealth of somebody else. We can develop the capability to give our personal wealth mentally, and we can also give what we own directly to others. However, we cannot give directly the wealth of others. For example, if we take somebody's treasured wealth and give it to somebody else who needs it, we will find ourselves in big trouble. But we can learn to give this kind of wealth mentally. Especially in tantric initiations, one goes through a section that says, "My body, speech, and mind, and also the belongings and wealth of myself as well as others, all of these I dedicate to others."

Between the belongings and the body, the body and its parts are much more difficult to give, so for the beginning practitioner, the giving of the body is not recommended at all. Particularly if you have the potential to achieve the higher path and realization with the help of the present body, then you are strongly discouraged from giving the body. Bodhisattvas at the higher level can give the body in two ways: one kind of bodhisattva experiences some pain when he is giving his body, whereas other bodhisattvas are free of pain when offering their body. Those bodhisattvas on the Path of Accumulation and the Path of Preparation do have pain or misery when they give their body. Even though there is a lot of pain involved, since it is for the sake of others, they gracefully accept it. In comparison, the *Bodhicaryavatara* says that those bodhisattvas who are on the tenth ground or *bhumi*, having the direct non-conceptual perception of emptiness, have no pain whatsoever, physically or mentally, in giving any parts of their body to others.

When we do the cutting meditation, or *chöd* practice, we invite all the hosts of spirits and mentally offer our body, fluids, bones, and everything to them. This is done on the imaginary level. We imagine that they all come as invited and enjoy our body, but we do not do it in a real sense. When we visualize ourselves as a deity, we know that we are not the deity at the present time, but due to the power of that visualization, we will become the deity in the future. So, the giving of our body, our wealth, and our merits, which we have earned, are earning, or will earn in the future—giving all of these, at least at the mental level, is very important to us. For instance, when we see somebody who is very sick and in terrible pain, even though we see only a single person who is going through this experience, we can learn to see that person as a representative of the entirety of sentient beings who are undergoing the same kind of torture at that very moment. On a personal level, we can use this as an opportunity to do something for every sentient being who is going through the same experience, by wishing that they could have a potion to eliminate every one of their problems. At the same time we should mentally create a potion filling the entire environment, and thus curing all similar problems. It would be very helpful if we could do that on at least the mental level.

We can train mentally to fulfill the wishes of those who are lacking food by giving them food, or those who are thirsty by giving something to drink, or those who are naked by giving clothes, or those who are without shelter by giving shelter, and so on. Try to fulfill every one of their needs mentally, to their complete satisfaction. Doing this thought training exercise again and again will increase our mental strength and capability. For that reason, the great Nagarjuna says in the *Precious Garland*, "To whomever the poison benefits or cures, please provide the poison." Notice that he does not say, "Give the poison to whomever wants the poison." If you were to provide poison to the peacock, it would thrive on it, but if we share the same thing with the crow, it will die. So, what we need to do is to check on whether whatever we give helps or not. If it seems to help, it should be done; if it seems to hurt, then it must not be done. For instance, giving a drink to an alcoholic does not work at all because it hurts that person. It is the same with giving a cigarette to a smoker. If what we are giving seems to help temporarily, but ultimately, it seems to hurt that person, then it must not be given. We must always check whether what we are trying to do is going to be helpful and not harmful. We have a willingness to help, but we also need the wisdom to see what is really helpful and what is not. If we see somebody who seems very desperate, using that desperation as our justification for giving them what seems to be their urgent need at that very moment could be wrong.

Verse Thirteen: Accepting the Negative Karma Of Others

*Although we're not guilty of any offenses*
*And never have harmed anyone in our lives,*
*If someone deluded should threaten to kill us*
*Because he is crazed with a tormented mind,*
*Then mercifully wishing for him not to suffer*
*From further misfortune because of his state,*
*We must take on ourselves the effects of his actions—*
*The Bodhisattvas all practice this way.*

The thirteenth verse says that accepting the negativities of those who inflict harm upon oneself is one of the practices of the bodhisattvas. For instance, if somebody wrongfully accuses us and then hits us even though the negative karma should belong to the other person, we should make a strong wish or aspiration to accept that negative karma as our own. Accepting such negative karma upon ourselves, through the strength of compassion, is one of the practices of the bodhisattvas. This is very straightforward and easy to understand. For example, if we are beaten nearly to death by somebody, without any wrongdoing on our part, the consequences for that other person will be disastrous when that karma matures. Understanding this, strong compassion arises, and we can accept that negative deed as part of our own negative karma. The capability to do this is one of the acts of the bodhisattvas. If someone takes our food away, the result for that person would be an existence in the hell, hungry ghost, or animal realms. Understanding how heavy the result of such an act can be, we develop strong compassion and become willing to accept that negative karma upon ourselves. Seeing what consequence could be in store for that other person, and therefore wishing that it will mature upon oneself, is one of the bodhisattva practices. If you have a very peaceful place to live, and then somebody wrongfully evicts you or takes your shelter away, the maturation of that action could be in one of the hell realms where the result is similar to the cause. Even in the human realm, that person could end up having difficulty finding shelter, wandering about without any place to stay and being homeless all of their life. Seeing that such heavy karma could fall upon that person due to their action of stealing your home, wishing to accept that negative karma upon yourself is one of the practices of the bodhisattvas.

I will give one more example. If somebody were to lie to us, cheat us, and even betray us, the result could be, at worst, a maturation in hell. But even if that person is born again as a human being, because the result is similar to the action, nobody will honor or trust the words of that person. Understanding the consequences of such an act, with strong compassion, again accepting the negative karma of the act upon ourself is one of the practices of the bodhisattvas. There are many sources for this practice, but the key one is the *Bodhicaryavatara* by Shantideva, which says, "May all the negativities of everyone else mature upon me, and may all my happiness and merits mature upon them." This practice is primarily derived from that line of the *Bodhicaryavatara*.

### Verse Fourteen: Returning Praise For Insult

*If someone insulting should spread ugly rumors*
*About us with cruel words unpleasant to hear,*
*And even if what he has said spreads to others*
*And gains wide acceptance as being the truth;*
*Yet out of our wish for the one who's maligned us*
*To conquer his troubles and gain peace of mind,*
*We must practice all virtues and treat him with kindness—*
*The Bodhisattvas all practice this way.*

The fourteenth bodhisattva practice is responding to words of insult with words of praise. When someone tries to harm us through insult or humiliation, reciprocating with words of praise or declaring that person's good qualities is one of the practices of the bodhisattvas. Even if somebody says enough unpleasant words against us to fill one hundred million worlds, respond with a mind of strong loving compassion, by praising their qualifications and saying pleasant words to them. There are four practices which make a person a virtuous or true practitioner. The first one is that even if we are insulted, not to insult in return. Of course, this kind of act does not come easily. It requires strong persistence in training. One of the reasons it is so difficult is that we have been training in how to give insults from the very beginning of our life, and because insulting comes so easily for us, it takes a very conscious effort not to engage in it.

Our instinct, if we are insulted by someone, is to say something twice as insulting to them. This is our habit from previous training, but we can put this behind us now. Of course, we do not have the training to say something nice to somebody who is insulting us constantly, so we have to begin that training now. Let us not postpone it until tomorrow or the day after tomorrow or next year. Let us say we will try to start right now. Of course, none of us are facing any major crisis of that kind at this moment but if an incident does occur, then instead of just repeating our past routine, let us just remind ourselves of what is advised here. That will be a good choice.

However, if you are not used to doing this, when somebody insults us and we praise them right away, they might even take it as a double insult because they are not used to taking that kind of compliment. In the past, we may not have returned their insult with harsh words, but we tended to hold a grudge, waiting for the moment when we could return the same favor. Instead, from now on, even if we do not give them a compliment right away, just wait until there is a gathering of friends or acquaintances and tell them what a wonderful person that person is, emphasizing that person's good qualities and giving him or her a compliment.

If we make it sound like we are giving a compliment but then talk about the negative deeds he has done, praising him for those actions, that is not the kind of compliment we are talking about here. We must not encourage anything bad he has done. For instance, if he has killed a large number of people in a war, and we compliment him on his bravery, that is not beneficial. Or if we complimented him on how much beer he was drinking, that compliment is not helpful. In a true sense that is not a compliment, but is really a insult. We have to give proper thought to what we say and try to be nice about it.

### Verse Fifteen: Seeing Enemies as Spiritual Teachers

*If we're in the midst of a large crowd of people*
*And someone should single us out for abuse,*
*Exposing our faults before all within hearing*
*And pointing out clearly the flaws we still have;*
*Then not getting angry nor being defensive,*
*Just listening in silence and heeding his words,*
*We must bow in respect to this man as our teacher—*
*The Bodhisattvas all practice this way.*

To be able to regard a person who is insulting us in front of a large gathering as a true spiritual master is one of the practices of the bodhisattvas. So, I have a story here. There was once a great Kadampa lama who was giving a teaching to a large gathering, and there was a woman who did not like him at all. She had a baby, and she brought the baby to the gathering and put him on the lap of the lama and said, "Please take back your baby. This is yours." The lama replied, "Thank you very much," and he took the baby. Truly, the person who creates a very embarrassing incident serves as a true spiritual master, in the sense that that person gives us a wonderful opportunity to develop our patience. If somebody insults us very badly in a gathering, shouting to everybody about what an awful person we are, and propagating the worst slander against us, then in return we must show strong patience and look up to that person as a true spiritual master. This is a big challenge, but it is one of the practices of the bodhisattvas.

As I mentioned earlier, there are four qualities of a true spiritual practitioner. Even if somebody criticizes us, we must not criticize in return. Even if somebody intentionally looks for our faults, we must not do so in return. Even if somebody gets angry with us, we must not get angry in return. Even if somebody hits us, we must not hit in return. These are the four practices which make a person a practitioner. Most of the time it is easy for us to declare ourselves dharma practitioners when no such circumstances arise, but under difficult circumstances, we can lose sight of that. It is important to remember these points every moment. If we keep these guidelines in mind and use them in our daily life, we will be able to keep the strong shield of patience and tolerance whenever we face attack by insulting words. Again, this is one of the essential practices of the bodhisattvas.

### Verse Sixteen: Giving Unconditional Love

*If someone we love and have cared for with kindness,*
*As an unselfish mother would cherish her child,*
*Should shun our devotion with thankless resentment*
*And treat us as if we're his most hated foe,*
*Then seeing these acts as a terrible sickness*
*Befallen our child and affecting his mind,*
*We must treat him with even more love and affection—*
*The Bodhisattvas all practice this way.*

If somebody whom I have taken care of and nurtured like my only child, in return looks upon me as an enemy, to continue to care for that person as if they were sick is one of the practices of the bodhisattvas. Just like a mother shows exceeding love and care, especially when the child is ill, so may we be able to cherish that person with ever increasing love. In the text, *Eight Verses on Thought Training* by Geshe Langri Tangpa, it says, "When someone I have benefited and in whom I have placed great trust hurts me very badly, I will practice seeing that person as my supreme teacher."

In this same context, Lama Tsongkhapa said, "May I treat anybody who says unpleasant words to me with excelling love, like a mother's love for her child." In various texts, different words or a different style of composition are used but, in fact, what it comes down to is the same point. If we take care of someone for many years and then they turn against us, that really makes us extremely angry. We get especially angry at that person for such behavior because we think, "I have done so much for that person. I am the one who is responsible for all his success and happiness and all the prosperity he has now." Thinking of those things makes you excessively angry about what that person is doing.

When anger is aroused as a result of such thinking, in place of anger, now we should be able to substitute exceptional love and compassion toward that person. We should learn to do this from now on, because we all, as ordinary sentient beings, are very vulnerable to this sort of incident. For instance, if we have helped someone and then we ask that person for a favor like, "Could you do such and such errand for me?" and that person says, "I am busy, I can't do it today," that makes us mad. The reason for the anger is that we helped that person earlier when he needed help, so now we expect to receive help in return. When we do not get it, anger arises. The advice states that we should try to reverse the anger by loving that person just like a mother cares for her only child. When we say to show loving kindness and motherly love to that person, that does not mean to go to his place and pamper him, but rather, to change the attitude in our heart to one of compassion rather than anger.

### Verse Seventeen: Remaining Humble When Criticized

*If by our own equals or those who are lower*
*In intellect, spiritual level, or wealth,*
*We're insulted and treated as if we were nothing*
*By the force of their pride and their jealous contempt,*
*Then seeing that they are like Gurus to teach us*
*To be always humble and conquer our pride,*
*We must treat them with honor and place them above us—*
*The Bodhisattvas all practice this way.*

If somebody abuses us or humiliates us, the humiliation or abuse that we receive should not cause us to be discouraged. Instead we should take courage and accept the responsibility for their actions. If the person who is trying to humiliate us is below us in status, we should not get discouraged but instead we should regard that person as our own teacher. When somebody who is equal or somebody who is below us, through their conceit or arrogance, tries to humiliate or insult us, accepting that person respectfully in the manner that we receive our own spiritual master is one of the practices of the bodhisattvas.

This is a difficult practice because when the person from whom we are receiving the insult is considered to be beneath us, or is even our equal, our arrogance makes the criticism harder to accept. Nevertheless, we have to learn to train our minds to make it easier. We get this opportunity everywhere. Especially at the workplace, if somebody who is less skilled than ourselves tries to abuse us or tries to override us, we become particularly indignant. Under such circumstances, we get much angrier than usual because we see that his skill, educational level, or level of responsibility is much below our own; we feel that an insult from such a person is undeserved. For instance, if a person who is equal to us in rank or job title tries to prevail over us or boss us around, then it makes us very angry because that person has no authority to do so. It especially makes us angry if a person who is below us gets a promotion and earns more money than we do. When such an incident actually does happen, our mind starts to bring forth all the improper reasons, one after the other, of why we should be mad. That is the moment we should learn not to hate or be angry with that person. That is the whole training.

Moreover, we have to realize how kind that person is to us. Since we all aspire to be enlightened, and since enlightenment is impossible without the help of sentient beings, that person becomes a remarkable force of enlightenment. In terms of providing us with the opportunity to attain enlightenment, that person is equal to the Buddha as well as to our own teacher. This point may not make too much sense right now and we may think it is not very practical. But if we think about it and get used to the idea, then gradually we will see some improvement and the right attitude will begin to grow.

### Verse Eighteen: Taking on the Suffering of Others

*If we are but men of most meager subsistence*
*And always receive a great deal of abuse,*
*If we find ourselves constantly gripped by much sickness*
*And experience harm, interruption and pain,*
*Then accepting ourselves all these hardships that others*
*Would have to have suffered from wrongs they had done,*
*We must never lose courage to take pain from others—*
*The Bodhisattvas all practice this way.*

The eighteenth verse says that even if we are constantly insulted or humiliated by others, in return we should share the responsibility of relieving their suffering and obstacles and help them attain enlightenment. This is one of the practices of the bodhisattvas. The seventeenth and eighteenth verses look similar, but there is a definite difference between the two. The seventeenth verse encourages us to regard a person who belittles us as our spiritual master; whereas the eighteenth verse says to be willing to accept their suffering and their negativities upon ourselves.

The eighteenth verse states that we should maintain the courage to continuously practice tonglen and not become disheartened even in the face of adversity. Bodhisatvas engage in tonglen even when being bombarded by insults; possessed by spirits or mental problems, illness, or fear; or even when lacking the basic necessities—like food, clothing, shelter or friends. Usually, if we don't have any food or drink then that is the time when we normally put aside our dharma practice and look for food. For instance, if we have some kind of headache or stomach discomfort that automatically causes us to decrease our dharma practice or postpone it for another day. Those things happen, but this section encourages us to give our dharma practice top priority—whether we are going through a happy time or a miserable time.

There is a Tibetan saying which illustrates this point, "When we are well fed and the climate is good, we look like a very accomplished yogi, but when adverse circumstances fall upon us, we become an ordinary person." When we encounter difficulties, we must not become any less of a yogi, but remain a yogi no matter what the circumstances. Another way of looking at it is that whatever bad thing happens to us, we should try to view them as something beneficial for our dharma practice. By turning difficulties to our advantage, they become the means to enable us to reach the goal, which is enlightenment. For that reason, in the *Seven Point Thought Training* by Geshe Chekawa, there is a special section where it says, "Transform adverse conditions into the path to enlightenment." Also, Panchen Lama Chökyi Gyeltsen's text, *Lama Chöpa*, says, "Though the world and the beings therein are full of the fruits of evil, and undesired sufferings shower upon me like rain, inspire me to see them as means of exhausting the results of negative karma, and to take these miserable conditions as a path."

We encounter difficult circumstances every day, and it is of some consolation to think about these things. When we see our ill circumstances, we mustn't make things worse by making ourselves unhappy. When we say "to be happy," we mean to make use of ill circumstances by transforming them into something conducive to attaining enlightenment. If we acquire the skill to do that, then we have reasons to be joyful.

### Verse Nineteen: Avoiding Arrogance

*Though praised and well-known and admired by many*
*Who act most respectful by bowing their heads,*
*Though having obtained a vast treasure of riches,*
*Which equals the store of the great God of Wealth,*
*Yet seeing full well that this fruit of samsara,*
*Though fortunate, still has no essence at all,*
*We must cast out what pride we might have in these glories—*
*The Bodhisattvas all practice this way.*

The nineteenth verse says if we become famous and wealthy, that should not cause us to become conceited or arrogant. One of the practices of the bodhisattvas is not to become arrogant or conceited under those circumstances. One of the dangers of becoming a famous celebrity is that we develop a callousness towards other sentient beings. When we see a lot of people drawn toward us, becoming our fans, it becomes very difficult not to have an inflated ego. For that reason, we must try to have a controlled mind.

When we are famous it becomes particularly difficult to return respect to those we see as being beneath us. Also, when we become wealthy, we become slightly arrogant. We might have a tendency to look down on other people or to insult them. If we achieve wealth or fame, we don't have to discard them. Instead, we need to learn to not have such a strong attachment to the words we hear from our admirers. Just treat the words as the sounds of the wind in a deserted area, and then they will not affect us. In addition, if many people pay us respect, returning their respect will help reduce our arrogance.

We may have gained lots of wealth, but that wealth is no more dependable than a dewdrop on the tip of a blade of grass. Even if I own some property today, who knows who will be the owner of this same property tomorrow. It is very uncertain. For example, a person could have a chest made out of gold and hold a golden key. However, something could happen overnight and the next morning that key could belong to somebody else. This example serves to show us that when we have wealth, the best thing is not to cling or become attached to that property, but show generosity towards those who have less. I would also like to quote from the Seventh Dalai Lama Kelsang Gyatso, who says, "A beautiful physique, youthfulness, and wealth are a few of the major sources of our arrogance."

His Holiness Kelsang Gyatso, the Seventh Dalai Lama, wrote *Praise to the Arya* to request Avalokiteshvara to connect all the beings with the chain of his compassion. He wrote this poem of praise in order to move the heart of Avalokiteshvara (the word Arya in the title refers to Avalokiteshvara). In one section of the text, it says that those who are high, sooner or later become the lowest of slaves who are stomped on. Those who have high status, which is translated as those who are brahmins, i.e. who have the highest samsaric status, like royalty, will eventually fall in status, and through changing rebirths may grow up to be slaves who are kicked around by some other master. Such things do happen, so there is no reason to be excessively attached to high status.

Beautiful physique and youthfulness are momentary and fade just like the autumn flower. That is easy to understand. These qualities are just like the lily that blossoms only for a single day and begins to wither the following day. If we think about this fact, attachment or arrogance will not develop. It is certain that what we have in this world will have to be given up eventually. The wealth we have in this life is just like a necklace that we have rented for a certain length of time. It is just a matter of time before it has to be returned. If we rent some ornaments and become very attached to them, that is a sign of low intelligence, especially if we get the attitude that this rented necklace is really ours. In a similar manner, this environment that we live in, the mountains, the green valleys, the ocean, our house, and our property—all these things, we think we own them, but in a true sense, do we really? We don't. Because they are all returned after a certain time.

The Dalai Lama says of our lifespan, "My life is like a flash of lightning; it too is momentary." His message is that because life is so short, it really is not worthwhile to spend it trying to secure friends and to eliminate the enemies of this life. If we use this short life for that end, then that is really worthless.

### Verse Twenty: Eliminating The Enemy Within

*If anger that dwells in our hearts lies neglected*
*And turning instead to our external foes,*
*We try to destroy them and even kill thousands,*
*Then thousands of others will plague us still more.*
*So seeing this action is not a solution,*
*Let's muster the forces of mercy and love;*
*Turn inwards and tame the wild flow of our mindstream—*
*The Bodhisattvas all practice this way.*

This verse says that combating our ill mental stream with the powerful alliance of compassion and love is one of the practices of the bodhisattvas. The battle we are going to wage is within. The force which wages the battle and the force which we are trying to conquer are both within us. This verse says that if we are unable to conquer our true inner enemy, which is our hatred, then no matter how much we overcome our external enemies, there will always be more. The forces of compassion and love that we are talking about here are not something that can be obtained from someone else. These are qualities we need to develop within us. Using the forces of love and compassion to abolish hatred is one of the practices of the bodhisattvas.

Shantideva's work, the *Bodhicaryavatara*, says if we have several acres of land filled with thorns, it would be very difficult to cover the entire surface with leather. But if we have very strong thongs on our feet made out of the leather of patience, then all the thorns are overcome. Let's say we have several enemies outside. It would take a long time to get rid of them if we faced them individually, one by one. However, if we conquer the hatred within us that is the enemy within, then all these external enemies will automatically disappear. The example of the feet and the thorn-covered land is a very helpful one. Moreover, all the writings of the *Bodhicaryavatara* by Shantideva are written from his own personal experiences. Likewise, most of the writings by the great Indian pandits, Tibetan scholars and yogis, up until now, are written from their own personal experiences.

In this context, the First Dalai Lama, Gendun Drub, wrote a poem titled *Song of the Eastern Snow Mountains*. Gendun Drub was the direct disciple and contemporary of Lama Tsongkhapa. Sometimes he would go to his birthplace, Tsang. One day, while he was in Tsang, he suddenly missed his lama, Lama Tsongkhapa, very much. So, he wrote a poem that says, "There is a white cloud on the tip of the mountain which seems to be trying to reach the sky. Just the sight of that cloud makes me miss my kind lama, and I am convinced of your kindness." In that poem, in one line he says, "Delusions are the enemy which stays within us, so conquer them."

Everyone here, including myself, should try with all available effort to work toward conquering the enemies that are within us. Truly speaking, the deluded mind inside us is the true enemy. To illustrate this, I will tell you a story about the great yogi, Milarepa. Once Milarepa was meditating in a cave that was dark inside and looked haunted. He had always been scared that one day something might come out of the dark and strike him. He thought, "Something dreadful is going to come out of that area and harm me." One day there appeared a dreadful, scary-looking ogre. Initially, Milarepa was terrified. Then realizing his terror, he stopped and started to investigate the evolution of the situation. He realized that it was his own mental fabrication, his own mental creation that had appeared at that moment. Because of that experience, he wrote a poem that says, "Unless your mind arises as an enemy, there is no reason for that ogre to come as an enemy." After Milarepa had recited the poem, he sat in contemplation and the ogre disappeared.

### Verse Twenty-One: Abandoning Sensory Indulgences

*Indulging in objects our senses run after*
*And drinking salt water are one and the same:*
*The more we partake, for our own satisfaction,*
*The more our desires and thirst for them grow.*
*Thus when we conceive a compulsive attraction*
*Toward whatever object our senses desire,*
*Abandon it quickly without hesitation—*
*The Bodhisattvas all practice this way.*

The twenty-first verse says that getting rid of those things that are the immediate causes of strong clinging and attachment is one of the practices of the bodhisattvas. All the beautiful appearances of the desire realm are like salty water. The objects of the five senses—form, sound, smell, taste, and touch—are all like salty ocean water. The more you drink salty water, the more your thirst increases. Instead of quenching your thirst, it makes it worse. In a similar manner, the more we indulge in these sensory objects, the more our attachment and hatred increase. In no way does indulging in these sensory objects allow us to reduce our attachment. For instance, if we love the beauty of a flower, first we like to look at one flower, but the next day we want a flower that is even more beautiful. Then we just look and shop around at all the florists to find a better flower. Or, for instance, if we are a music lover, then we keep listening to music and we always hope to hear better music. This love of music makes us spend lots of money buying compact discs and going to concerts. And it's not only the money; time is consumed in the process, and all that time is wasted just by an attachment to sound. Some people feel they have to buy records, and when they have to move or relocate, their biggest problem is how to move the records that they've bought over the years.

If we have a craving for smells, we spend a lot of time and energy trying to find a perfect scent. We are never satisfied but keep buying one fragrance after another. We go from one shop to the other, spending lots of time, just looking for the perfect smell. This is a result of the craving for smell. If we have a craving for taste, then we check out all sorts of restaurants, but our craving just increases. For instance if we had one really good meal, then we do not say, "Okay, that is enough." No, we have to have something better. This is the way that the craving for taste keeps growing. There is no end to it. Of course, we need to use the powers of our five senses, but we should use them in moderation. We need to have some sense of contentment, so that we don't waste too much time and energy chasing after sense objects. Since we are extremely vulnerable to attachment, the author encourages us to give up craving for or clinging to the five kinds of sensory objects. This is one of the practices of the bodhisattvas.

### Verse Twenty-Two: Dispelling Belief in Inherent Existence

*Whatever appears to be truly existent*
*Is just what our mind in delusion creates;*
*This mind of ours also is, from the beginning,*
*Devoid of an essence inherently real.*
*Then seeing that Truth is beyond the conceptions*
*We have of the known and the knower as well,*
*Dispel the belief in inherent existence—*
*The Bodhisattvas all practice this way.*

There are two kinds of entities: objective things and the mind which apprehends them. The twenty-second verse says that to perceive neither objective nor subjective forms as existing on their own is one of the practices of the bodhisattvas. Whatever appears to us originates in our mind. But the mind itself, which is the origin, lacks true existence from the very beginning. This line literally says not to perceive these things in the mind, but that does not mean not to perceive them at all. It just means not to perceive them as being truly or independently self-existent.

Luminosity is the very nature of our mind. The nature of our mind is undefiled by the stain of thoughts, and those stains or dirt are not inseparable from our mind. Of course, our luminous mind is obscured temporarily by external stains, but the obscurations are not within the mind itself. Maitreya said in his *Uttaratantra*, "The very nature of mind is luminous and all stains thereon are temporary or adventitious."

All the stains or defilements are temporary or adventitious and thus are not part of the nature of mind itself. Therefore, we can be enlightened. An illustration of this is a coat with dirt on it. The coat is dirty, but the dirt can be cleaned off, since the dirt is not inseparable from the coat itself. If the defilements are inseparable from the mind itself, then there is no chance to be enlightened. If we accept the belief that the defilement has entered into the mind and is one with the mind, then when we remove the defilement, we would also remove the mind with it. But this is not the case.

### Verse Twenty-Three: Seeing Attractive Objects as Rainbow-Like

*Whenever we meet with a beautiful object,*
*Or something attractive that pleases our mind,*
*Then do not be fooled into thinking it differs*
*In fact from a summertime rainbow;*
*Though both of them have such a lovely appearance,*
*There's nothing substantial behind this facade.*
*Abandon the drives of compulsive attraction—*
*The Bodhisattvas all practice this way.*

The twenty-third verse says that even if captivating objects or people appear to us, not clinging to or grasping for them is one of the practices of the bodhisattvas. If we truly understand this, then staying in a big city like Los Angeles is no problem at all. Most of the time we believe that if we live in big cities, then we are vulnerable to all the attachments, hatred, and ignorance that run rampant. If we hold that notion, then we are on the wrong track, because we are believing that all these things come from outside, not from inside. Many of us have that notion, but that's not true at all. If we do not have these two factors, clinging and attachment, staying in a big city is no problem.

Just like a rainbow, an object might appear very beautiful to our eye. If we try to reach or grasp for it, it disappears. We cannot get hold of it. The fact that things do appear very beautiful to us is mostly due to our own false mental perception. We believe that the attractive qualities of that object are inherent in it. Actually, there is no independent existence on the part of that quality separate from our perception of it. One might argue that this is not a good example because the rainbow cannot be touched, whereas the objects that we find very attractive can be touched and sensed. The similarity between these two is in the way they are dependent upon certain causes. The rainbow is contingent upon two main circumstances coming together, light and moisture. When light and moisture occur in the air at the same time, a rainbow appears. Other attractive objects are also the result of many circumstances and conditions coming together, causing the object to appear attractive. However, there is no inherent attractiveness existing independently at all. Take the example of a car. There is no beautiful car existing independently of its parts or of our perception of it. The car is just a composite of many conditions coming together to which we impute existence as a beautiful car.

### Verse Twenty-Four: Seeing Undesirable Things as Illusory

*The various ills in our life that we suffer*
*Resemble the death of our child in a dream;*
*To hold as the truth what is merely illusion*
*Is needless exhaustion of body and mind.*
*For this very reason, when faced with unpleasant*
*Conditions that normally cause us much grief,*
*Approach them as if they were only illusion—*
*The Bodhisattvas all practice this way.*

The twenty-fourth verse says that whenever we encounter suffering or undesirable things, to perceive them as an illusion is one of the practices of the bodhisattvas. All types of suffering that we experience are the result of erroneous perception, just like in a dream. If we have dreamt of losing one of our siblings or our only child, it is painful, but it is all just an erroneous appearance. The suffering, pain, and anxiety we experience in a dream are still true even though the events are not really happening. Sometimes we even cry, and we find our pillow wet the next morning. Sometimes we find something very humorous in a dream and we laugh, even waking up the person next to us.

In this context, let me quote Shantideva from the *Bodhicaryavatara* where he says: "All the appearances of suffering which are experienced by the denizens of hell are the result of erroneous perception, but due to the influence of karma it becomes real to whoever faces it." Due to their bad karma, it becomes real for those people. The creator of the glowing iron surface of hell, which seems to last for centuries, is merely our own negative mind. The buddhas explain how those appearances are all the result of our negative mind.

In our case, we are unable to see illusion as illusion, but perceive it as truly existent. Due to this, problems start. Therefore, we should pray, "From now on, may I be able to apprehend erroneous appearances as they are." In the *Lama Chöpa*, it says, "Seeing all things, internal and external as illusory, like a dream or the reflection of the moon on a clear lake. Even though they do appear, through seeing that they lack inherent existence, may I be able to complete the illusion-like contemplation of samadhi."

### Verse Twenty-Five: Perfecting Generosity

*The beings who strive to be fully enlightened*
*Would give up their bodies pursuing this aim;*
*With this high example, what need is the mention*
*Of gifts we should make of the objects we have.*
*Without any hopes of return for our kindness,*
*Or thinking about all the merit we gain,*
*Engage in the practice of generous giving—*
*The Bodhisattvas all practice this way.*

The twenty-fifth verse is about practicing generosity without expecting anything in return. If those who aspire to enlightenment give even their own body, then we do not need to mention the external wealth that we need to give. What generosity is really about is the development of our power of giving. There are four types of generosity which we can practice: first, the practice of giving wealth; second, the giving of teachings—sharing the knowledge; third, the generosity of love; and fourth, the generosity of providing protection to someone.

Among these four, the most supreme is the generosity of the dharma. We may not have anything, not even a single penny, but still one may practice the generosity of sharing the dharma with others. When we contemplate the idea of sharing the dharma, we might feel, "No way can I teach dharma." I do not think that is the right notion. For instance, when we say our own prayers, just increase the volume so that the words may be heard by the beings in the vicinity, with the intent that it is meant as a form of dharma generosity and with the hope that it will benefit them. This in itself is a form of generosity. When we are alone in a park or on the street and we see animals or birds, then try to say some mantra, the name of a deity, or the name of the Buddha in the hope that it will benefit them. That in itself is a form of generosity. For instance, we must not ignore the population of ants, thinking that they are excluded; they are not. We can go near their nest and say some names of the Buddha which they can hear. Even if we do not have the power to change or to benefit those ants directly, certainly the names of the buddhas that we say for them will have some effect.

We can also practice generosity by giving our belongings to others. But if we try to give something by stealing or cheating, that is impure generosity. We do own our body, but to be able to give one's own body for all mother sentient beings is one of the most difficult things to do. We may not be able to give it directly, but we can imagine that we are giving our body to others. If we think that somebody needs something that we do not have, we can visualize or imagine we are mentally giving it to that person.

When we practice generosity, we should never, ever think of the fruition of that karma for ourselves. We must not think "What do I gain by this practice? What fabulous maturations are bound for me?" Such thoughts make the act of giving impure. However, one thing we must not forget is always to dedicate our merit: "By the virtue of the practice of this generosity, may we all attain the great enlightenment." This dedication prayer must be made after every practice. When we aspire to attain great enlightenment due to generosity, we talk about the fruition or the maturation, or the result of our karma. However, enlightenment is not the result of karma, but rather the result of accumulation of merit. For example, Milarepa did not own anything, but he did perform limitless acts of generosity every single day. He even said in one of his poems, "I do not have any material offerings for my gurus, but the kindness of my guru I will repay with my meticulous practice of the teachings." The best offering we can make is the offering of our own practice. That is the supreme act of generosity.

### Verse Twenty-Six: Perfecting Morality

*If lacking strict moral control of our conduct*
*We haven't been able to reach our own goals,*
*How can we fulfill all the wishes of others?*
*Undisciplined effort is surely absurd!*
*We have to renounce first attachment to pleasures*
*Which binds us so tightly to samsara's wheel,*
*Then protect all our vows of sworn moral behavior—*
*The Bodhisattvas all practice this way.*

The twenty-sixth bodhisattva practice is the cultivation of morality without any intention for samsaric achievement. Without morality, we cannot achieve our personal goal, so that makes trying to achieve something for others a joke. Our goal is comprised of two things: one is to accomplish our personal achievement, and the other is to accomplish the welfare of others. To achieve either of these two, all of our practice must be based on proper morality. This is clearly set forth by the Buddha in the Pratimoksha Sutra, which says, "Just as a person without legs cannot run, a person without proper morality cannot gain freedom from cyclic existence." All the praises and advantages of morality are spelled out by the Buddha in great detail in the Pratimoksha Sutra. For instance, if we live in a monastery, every fifteen days we have to do what they call confession, and we listen to the Pratimoksha Sutra.

What is morality? The real definition of morality is the desire or willingness to refrain from wrongdoings. Morality serves as a wall that blocks the flow of wrongdoings. When we achieve the virtue of morality, the inflow of all future wrongdoings is blocked. There are specific codes of moral discipline pertaining to the pratimoksha vows, the bodhisattva vows, and the tantric vows. But even if we have not taken any of these vows, we still need to practice natural morality by abstaining from the ten non-virtuous activities.

## Verse Twenty-Seven: Perfecting Patience

*For all Bodhisattvas with minds set on merit*
*Who wish to amass a great store of good deeds,*
*Encounters with those causing harm and destruction*
*Which test their commitment are mines of great wealth.*
*For this very reason, abandon resentment*
*And anger directed toward those who do harm;*
*Perfect meditation on patient endurance—*
*The Bodhisattvas all practice this way.*

Cultivating patience, instead of hatred, for those who harm us is the twenty-seventh bodhisattva practice. You have already heard a lot about patience, but here patience is compared to a treasure. A person who finds a treasure, would be extremely happy because of the instant wealth. Whenever those who long for the riches of virtue meet someone inflicting harm, it is like finding a great treasure because it provides the opportunity to practice patience. It becomes a source of great joy for that person. Thus, we can give up hatred and instead generate thoughts of patience toward all sentient beings. In the *Lam-Rim Chenmo*, Lama Tsongkhapa says that generosity is like the wish-granting gem which fulfills the wishes of all others; whereas he analogizes morality to cooling water that dissipates the heat of negative mental states. The wish-fulfilling gem is generosity, the cooling effect on the heat of negative mental states is morality, and the perfect ornament is patience.

Patience is the most perfect ornament for those who are strong. The effect of patience starts in our immediate home with whomever we live. If we live with our teacher, it begins with the teacher. At home, it starts with our children and spouse; and from home it goes out to the neighborhood. If we understand the devastating effect of hatred or anger, then we will have no problem contemplating patience.

Of course, the biggest effect of anger is that it leads us to the hell realms. Also, all the virtue that we have gained and that is not yet dedicated toward enlightenment is destroyed by a single moment of anger. Particularly if our anger is directed toward one of our siblings or toward our teacher, the result is extremely heavy. If we get angry with our father or mother or with sick people who are in a feeble state, the result is also quite heavy. The magnitude of the effect of anger depends on the object of the anger. If the object of our anger is a source of enormous kindness to us, that anger becomes disastrous. With the sick person, the point is that because that person is in a feeble condition, our getting angry can be very harmful, even though they may not have been kind to us. Of course, the disintegration of friendships is often caused by anger. Anger can be traced to most breakups between parents, siblings, spouses, or friends, because once the blaze of anger flares up we have difficulty cooling it down. Anger starts many of these conflicts and eventually leads to disunity among people. If we meditate on the demerits of anger, we will have no problem cultivating patience.

Patience does not just mean to be able to tolerate provocation without anger. Patience is far more than that. For instance, if we go through immense hardship in the process of our practice, tolerating that hardship is also a form of patience. When bodhisattvas have to perform extremely difficult feats, they accept every hardship with grace and eagerness. That is one kind of patience. We all have trouble tolerating hardships that we face in the process of our daily practice. For example, when we have a rough day at work, we are exhausted by the time we come home; then when we sit down to do our practice we want to make it go quickly, and shorten it wherever possible. This is a true sign that we have no tolerance for hardship.

We can endure these hardships by saying, "No matter what happens or how hard it might prove to be, I cannot compromise this practice. I must do it to the best of my capability, to fulfill the responsibility for my own personal progress, as well as the responsibility I have assumed for others. I cannot compromise." With that kind of attitude, we can try to tackle the difficult moments every single day and make our dharma practice a top priority. The positive result of tolerating such hardship is great. So, it's worth the effort to maintain patience at all times.

### Verse Twenty-Eight: Perfecting Enthusiastic Perseverance

*If Shravakas as well as Pratyekabuddhas,*
*Who work toward Nirvana for only themselves,*
*Exert so much effort fulfilling their purpose*
*That were they in flames they'd not budge from their goal,*
*Then how much more energy must be expended*
*By those of us working for everyone's sake;*
*Enlightenment calls for the most perseverance—*
*The Bodhisattvas all practice this way.*

The twenty-eighth bodhisattva practice is cultivating enthusiastic perseverance for the benefit of all other sentient beings. This text says even those shravakas or pratyekabuddhas who work for their own attainment, work at it eagerly. If our hair were on fire we would work fast to put out the fire. We would not sit still for even a moment, but would put it out as soon as we could. The shravakas and pratyekabuddhas who work only for their personal gain, work that hard with much enthusiastic perseverance; we who are working for the attainment of great enlightenment for the sake of all sentient beings, no doubt need to work that hard or even harder.

What is enthusiastic perseverance? Enthusiastic perseverance is the keen interest in doing what is virtuous. In America, we frequently use the term "energy." But, I think that enthusiastic perseverance and energy are a little bit different. "Energy," as I understand it, is almost like courage. So we can have courage to do both good things and bad things.

We could have worked very hard doing something negative, even working up a sweat, but that sweat is not the result of enthusiastic perseverance. Even if you wipe sweat off your forehead, that sweat is not due to enthusiastic perseverance. "Enthusiastic perseverance" literally means "fondness for performing virtuous acts." This is important for all of us, because we need all of the attainments that stem from enthusiastic perseverance, every one of them.

Chandrakirti, in his book the *Madhyamakavatara*, said all knowledge follows from enthusiastic perseverance. Also, Lama Tsongkhapa writes in the *Lam-Rim Chenmo*, "If we don the unchangeable armor of enthusiastic perseverance, then knowledge will increase within us like a waxing moon." That is why Chandrakirti and Lama Tsongkhapa encourage us to keep our interest going like a stream of water. It cannot be sporadic or intermittent; we must not be interested for a couple of days or so and then give up. Instead, we need to have persistence, maintaining continuity from month to month and year to year. It is

important to energize our everyday practice and daily good works
with enthusiasm, without anyone else telling us to, but doing it for
our own sake.

### Verse Twenty-Nine: Perfecting Concentration

*Higher insight that penetrates right to the essence,*
*Revealing the true way in which things exist,*
*Can only root out our emotional problems*
*If mental quiescence is laid as its base.*
*So exceeding the four formless states of absorption*
*We must work to achieve single-minded control*
*And the full concentration of deep meditation—*
*The Bodhisattvas all practice this way.*

The twenty-ninth verse says that meditating on samadhi (concentration), which goes beyond the four formless realms, is one of the
practices of the bodhisattvas. Calm abiding (shamatha) is the mind
that is single-pointedly focused on its object. The mind which com-
bines calm abiding with penetrating insight (vipashyana) can conquer
all negative mental states. For these reasons, contemplation on
samadhi, or single-pointed concentration, that transcends the four
formless realms, is one of the practices of the bodhisattvas.

Most of the time, contemplation on the development of samadhi
results in a rebirth in the formless realm. If our effort to develop calm
abiding is in the hope of attaining any of the formless existences, then
that is of no use to us. We have to achieve calm abiding for the sake of
something that transcends that hope. In one of the sutras, the Buddha
says that the bodhisattvas have no desire to be born in the formless
realms because beings there cannot see each other; so this is not a suit-
able place for dharma practice. The formless realm is actually one of
the eight places lacking in freedom where we do not want to be born.

They belong in the same category as the realm of the long-life gods who have no opportunity for dharma practice.

What is calm abiding or shamatha? Calm abiding means the placement of a single-pointed mind on an object. This is a tool we all must possess. In order to obtain that tool, we need to meditate on its development. With the aid of calm abiding, combined with penetrative insight, we can achieve our goal. We need penetrative insight to do the analysis. So, penetrative insight (the wisdom of emptiness or *shunyata*) is like a sharp weapon, and calm abiding is like a strong man with very solid shoulders. If we use penetrative insight with the help of calm abiding, then we can effectively cut the very root of all negative mental states, which are the source of all the afflictions.

These days a lot of people are interested in calm abiding meditation, but if we just take up this alone without insight meditation, the meditation of calm abiding itself becomes one of the means for wandering about within cyclic existence. By penetrating insight we are not talking about something which just blocks the gross negative mental states, but a fine penetrating insight that is capable of cutting the very root of the grasping of ego. On its own, calm abiding does not provide us with any means to break free from cyclic existence. Calm abiding itself is not unique to Buddhism and can be found in other religious traditions as well. For example, there are a lot of Hindus who accomplish calm abiding by meditating on the stages of samadhi. With that samadhi mind, they are then able to take birth in the form realm or in the formless realm. With the help of calm abiding, one can temporarily get rid of the gross negative mental states of the desire realm and even those of the form realm, thereby taking rebirth in the formless realm. With calm abiding one can progress even to the summit of cyclic existence, which is the highest among the four formless realms. People who have temporarily overcome all the gross negative mental states of the form realm and the desire realm often feel they have gained permanent freedom from their negative mental states and there is no longer anything left to be eradicated. They feel they have attained liberation. But once again, the karma necessary to be in that realm eventually runs out. When it does, those in that realm see the next place where they are about to take rebirth, which is where they began. This great disappointment causes them to lose faith in the dharma because they thought they had gained total freedom. When they find they are not yet free, they develop a distorted or harsh view of the dharma. This causes them to fall even further down into the lower realms.

Lama Tsongkhapa says that samadhi, or concentration, is like the king who completely governs the mind. When the mind is placed on any sort of object with that kind of concentration, it remains unmoved like a huge Mount Meru. That concentration, if directed to any kind of virtuous focal point, will follow that point without becoming sidetracked. Because of the virtue of calm abiding, both our body and mind will remain in an extremely workable state, inducing great mental bliss. If you are serious about meditating on calm abiding, you can achieve it in six months. There are, however, instances of some people trying it for three months—even three years, five years, or six years—but gaining nothing. Some claim that they have been meditating on calm abiding, and when you ask them how long, they say about six years, but still they have no control over their mind. Actually, I think in those cases, it's not really the calm abiding meditation that is at fault, but it is their personal approach that is at fault.

Verse Thirty: Perfecting Wisdom

*Perfection of charity, patience, and morals,*
*Absorption and effort just isn't enough;*
*Without the Perfection of Wisdom these five are*
*Unable to bring us to full Buddhahood.*
*With the methods of pure Bodhichitta develop*
*The wisdom to see that the actor, the act,*
*And the acted upon lack inherent existence—*
*The Bodhisattvas all practice this way.*

The thirtieth verse says that without *prajna* or wisdom, we cannot attain great enlightenment even if we have perfected all five of the other perfections, or *paramitas*. But wisdom cannot work on its own. It must be paired with the method, which is bodhicitta and compassion. The three spheres are the object, the agent, and the action performed. Understanding that all three lack inherent existence is wisdom. Combining wisdom with method is one of the practices of the bodhisattvas.

For instance, if we take the example of samadhi, the meditator him or herself is the agent, samadhi is the object, and the contemplation of samadhi is the action. The mind that realizes the lack of inherent existence of all three of these is the wisdom mind. Wisdom here is the realization of the subject. In Tibetan it is called *so sor*, which is individually, and *tok pa*, which is to comprehend, so wisdom is the comprehension of subjects individually. In the *Bodhicaryavatara*, it says that the first five perfections are the methods that help us to induce the sixth perfection, wisdom. All these first five perfections were taught by the Buddha for the sake of understanding wisdom, the sixth perfection, or paramita. This can be found in the ninth chapter of the *Bodhicaryavatara* by Shantideva.

I think we need to make an effort every day to find out about the sixth paramita, the wisdom paramita. Try hard to get close to understanding it. Wisdom is the tool that truly destroys the grasping of the ego. Particularly, in order to overcome obscurations that block the direct knowledge of all things, wisdom must be supported by the method, the five other paramitas. For instance, the shravakas and pratyekabuddhas have the wisdom of emptiness, but due to lack of method, they have no means with which they can effectively oppose the obscurations which block the direct knowledge of things.

### Verse Thirty-One: Getting Rid of Faults

*Without making efforts to analyze clearly*
*Delusions we have and mistakes we commit,*
*Then even though outwardly practicing Dharma,*
*We still may perform many non-Dharma deeds.*
*For this very reason, let's try to examine*
*Mistakes and delusions and faults we possess,*
*And afterwards try to remove them completely—*
*The Bodhisattvas all practice this way.*

The thirty-first bodhisattva practice is observing and investigating faults in our daily living and getting rid of them. If we do not investigate or observe our own errors and faults, we may possibly perform a non-dharma act in the guise of the dharma. For that reason, in our daily living, we need to observe our own errors or mistakes; not only observe them, but whenever we see them, either block them or try to eliminate them. Trying to eliminate those faults is one of the practices of the bodhisattvas.

I think I recommended on several occasions that we observe our activities of body, speech, and mind, and whenever we notice something that is wrong, learn to drop it. I have commented on that many times. One method is to check our actions three times a day. At about noon, look back on the day's events in the morning and check, "Have

I done anything wrong or have I done something good?" If we have done something good or virtuous then we can encourage ourselves to do more, but if we have done something wrong that we would regret, we should purify it. When we are leaving work, we can sit in our car before driving home and check on what we have done between lunchtime and the time we got off work. We should make a list of what we have done, and if we have done something right, then we can rejoice in that act. If we have done something wrong, then we should regret what we have done. Then, just before going to bed, we should review our actions and see what we have done that day.

### Verse Thirty-Two: Avoiding Bringing Up Others' Faults

*While speaking of others, the force of delusion*
*May cause us to talk of the flaws they possess;*
*If those we find fault in should be Bodhisattvas,*
*Our own reputation will suffer instead.*
*So don't run the risk of disparaging others*
*Who've entered upon Mahayana's great path;*
*Only the faults that we have should we mention—*
*The Bodhisattvas all practice this way.*

The thirty-second verse says that one who has embarked on the Mahayana path should not bring up the faults of others, especially if the other person is a bodhisattva. If someone has done something wrong or has some fault and that person chooses to conceal it, then that is their business. It is not our responsibility to declare their faults. On the other hand, if we have done something wrong, we need to declare that wrongdoing, confess it, and purify it. Whether we declare anybody else's fault doesn't matter. In fact, if we bring up the faults of another who is actually one of the bodhisattvas, due to our own negative mental states, we will impair ourselves.

Even if that person is not one of the bodhisattvas, like one of our co-workers, there is no reason to bring up their faults unnecessarily. Also, if we see faults in our parents or siblings, we should just ignore them and not bring them up; that is wise. If there is a very good reason why their fault should be brought up, then certainly do so, particularly if we can be a witness in a trial. When we know that person has committed a crime, then we should stand up and speak. However, if it seems that our honesty will endanger the other person's life, then we may evade it. This is important.

### Verse Thirty-Three: Abandoning Attachment to Households

*Domestic disputes with our friends and relations,*
*To gain their respect or the things we feel due,*
*Will leave us unable to listen to Dharma,*
*Unable to study or meditate well.*
*Since danger is found in the homes of our patrons,*
*As well as in those of our family and friends,*
*Abandon attachment we have to have to these households—*
*The Bodhisattvas all practice this way.*

This verse says that giving up attachment to our parents' home or the home of our sponsor is one of the practices of the bodhisattvas. Why do we need to give up attachment to our home or our benefactor's home? If we keep on clinging to them, then a quarrel may arise over what services or offerings are expected, and such conflict will impair our studies and meditation. If we stay attached to the home of our relatives or sponsors, what happens is whenever there is a conflict, we try to intervene, so we start minding their business. Our business is actually the study and practice of the dharma.

I have witnessed that problem several times in my lifetime. I had some benefactors, but whenever I visited them, I just paid attention to my own memorization and chanting of prayers. I never interfered in their business. Sometimes I had the urge to mind their business, but my sponsor was a very wonderful person who would not let me mingle with them. He would always leave me in the shrine. The reason is that if those things interfere with our studies, contemplation, and meditation—our primary aim—then certainly that interference is not worthwhile at all. For that reason, we should give up attachment to our sponsor's home, or girlfriend's home, or boyfriend's home, and not have any attachment. Rather, we should regard those homes as guest houses. That is a wise thing to do. For instance, if we were renting a room in a motel, we would never interfere in the management or the business of the motel. In a similar manner, we should have the same kind of attitude whenever we visit our benefactors or friends. That would be best.

### Verse Thirty-Four: Not Returning Harsh Words

*The words of abuse that we utter in anger*
*Cause others much pain by disturbing their minds;*
*And we who are striving to be Bodhisattvas*
*Will find that our practice will surely decline.*
*So seeing the faults that arise from harsh language,*
*Which those who must hear find unpleasant to bear,*
*Abandon abuse that's directed toward others—*
*The Bodhisattvas all practice this way.*

The thirty-fourth bodhisattva practice is not to return the harsh words we receive from others. Harsh words are unpleasant to hear, no matter who speaks them. That is why we never want to speak harsh words to anybody. Rough language will disturb the hearts of others.

If their minds are disturbed, then that will undermine our own bodhisattva practice. One of the practices of the bodhisattvas is never speaking any words that are harsh to the heart of others. Any words that really disturb the mind of another person, cause anger in their mind or aggravate their suffering, are words that we always want to avoid in our daily language. Harsh words are like an arrow that strikes right to the heart. So, we should make a very conscious effort never to exchange harsh words, no matter to whom we are talking, whether that person is higher, equal, or very humble. Never using any harsh words with anyone should be our constant effort.

### Verse Thirty-Five: Eliminating Bad Habits

*Defiled types of actions will soon become habits*
*As we grow accustomed to base states of mind;*
*A great deal of effort will then be required*
*For the force of opponents to counter these stains.*
*So armed with the weapons alertness and memory,*
*Attack such defilements as lust on first sight;*
*Remove these obstructions that hinder our progress—*
*The Bodhisattvas all practice this way.*

The thirty-fifth verse says that whenever we notice the early rise of attachment and negative mental states, we should overcome them. We need to control them at the earliest stage possible, because if we welcome our negative mental states and allow them to stay for a while, then we acquire a habit that will grow. If we do not control negative mental states, it becomes much harder to oppose them. We need to use mindfulness and alertness to keep very close surveillance on any that arise. Sometimes we deliberately do something wrong, but we often have an excuse such as, "I know it is wrong, but I want to experiment." If we welcome that kind of mind, then the longer it stays, the more it grows out of control. For instance, if others say, "I know you don't drink or smoke, but why don't you just experiment, just this one time?" We can say, "No thank you; it doesn't help." As we know, if there is a war, it is more effective to stop the invader right at the border, but if we don't, they come in and colonize the entire country. Then getting rid of them is much more difficult. The best thing to do is to stop them right at the border.

### Verse Thirty-Six: Being Alert

*In short, then whatever we do in whatever*
*Condition or circumstance we might confront*
*Should be done with the force of complete self-awareness,*
*Which comprehends fully the state of our mind.*
*Then always possessing alertness and memory,*
*Which keep us in focus and ready to serve,*
*We must work for the welfare of all sentient beings—*
*The Bodhisattvas all practice this way.*

The thirty-sixth verse says that maintaining alertness in our daily efforts to benefit others is one of the practices of the bodhisattvas. The welfare of others is very important and to help effectively we need to be mindful and mentally alert. In every action of our body, speech, and mind, watch closely with mental alertness, and never allow any of these three to engage in negativity.

### Verse Thirty-Seven: Dedicating All Merit

*All merits we gain from the efforts we're making*
*To put into practice these virtuous ways,*
*Which we do for the sake of removing the suffering*
*Endured by the limitless mothers we've had,*
*We must dedicate purely for them to be Buddhas,*
*With wisdom that sees that both they and ourselves*
*As well as this merit all lack true existence—*
*The Bodhisattvas all practice this way.*

The thirty-seventh bodhisattva practice is dedicating all virtue that we create for great enlightenment for the benefit of the limitless number of sentient beings. In this verse it says that all the virtues we have gathered, through enthusiastic perseverance, eradicate the negative mental states and sufferings of limitless sentient beings. Employing the wisdom that is free from grasping after true existence of the three objects, and dedicating merit for great enlightenment together form one of the practices of the bodhisattvas.

### Conclusion

*By carefully following all of the teachings*
*My most holy Gurus have given to me*
*Concerning the meanings of sutra and tantra*
*Explained by the Buddhas and masters of old,*
*I've written this work on the practices numbering*
*Thirty and seven of all Buddhas' Children*
*To benefit those who desire to follow*
*The path that all Bodhisattvas must tread.*

*Because of my poor intellectual powers*
*And meager amount of the training I've had,*
*I haven't been able to write polished verses*
*In meter and style that would please those with skill;*
*But as I've relied on the words of the sutras*
*And all that my most holy Gurus have taught,*
*I'm certain that this is without any errors;*
*This truly is what Buddhas' Children have all done.*

*However, because the extent and the depth*
*Of the great waves of conduct of all Buddhas' Children*
*Are hard to be fathomed by someone of limited*
*Powers of intellect as is myself,*
*There are bound to be faults, contradictions in meaning,*
*Disjointed connections and many such flaws;*
*So most holy Gurus, I beg your indulgence,*
*Be patient with all the shortcomings I have.*

These are the thirty-seven major practices of the bodhisattvas, which are described here in a very condensed form by the bodhisattva Togmey Zangpo. These are the direct practices of the bodhisattvas, but indirectly they are meant for anyone who has the Mahayana seed within and has decided to become a Mahayana practitioner. Even though some of these practices may not work as powerfully as we would like, or may not be as effective as those of the bodhisattvas, we can still try to come close to what a bodhisattva would do.

The author states that he wrote this according to the scriptures taught in both the Sutra and Tantra, following the holy speech of the masters. He has presented these thirty-seven verses in order to help those who aspire to become bodhisattvas. In the last two stanzas, the author speaks about his limited understanding and asks for the patience of his teachers. This is a way of reducing his own arrogance and pride.

### Dedication

*With pure Bodhichitta of ultimate voidness,*
*Yet relative nature of mercy and love,*
*Devoid of extremes of this worldly existence*
*And passive absorption in blissful release,*
*May all sentient beings receiving the merit*
*Amassed by the effort I've made in this work*
*Soon reach your attainment, great Lokeshvara,*
*All-seeing protector with love for us all.*

Lastly is the dedication of the merit that the author has gained from writing this text. It is very important for us to dedicate our merit at the end of our meditation session or after any dharma activity. We have now concluded the entire text.

## DEDICATION OF MERIT

Due to the virtue or merit that has been received by doing any type of dharma action, may His Holiness the Dalai Lama and all the great holy masters who preserve and promote the teachings live for a very long time. May the whole sangha community existing throughout the world abide in pure morality, be free from any quarrel or schism, and be successful in their studies and contemplations. May all the nations of the world be free from war, illness, famine, and conflict. May peace prevail and endure forever on this earth. May all sentient beings become free of the suffering of samsara and attain lasting peace, happiness and great enlightenment.

# Questions and Answers

Q: Sometimes dharma practitioners do these things to me, and I feel like they are trying to test me. But I feel like it is demeaning to them to use these methods—like to insult me in public to test my patience as a dharma practitioner.

A: If these things happen, learning to ignore them is very important. Sometimes it may not be coming from the other person, but it could be a reflection of our own self on the other person. We never know whether that is truly coming from the other person or if it is a reflection of our own thinking. So, we have to analyze that properly. For instance, even though you mean no harm to anybody, someone else might find you in that awkward place you described. They might find some things you do insulting to them. We all may find part of ourselves in certain circumstances.

Q. Geshe-la, I feel we practice the least when we dwell on something that hurt us or something that happened to us that makes us angry and we hold on to it. Is there a meditative practice to release it, to release whatever we have taken on?

A. Of course there are meditations. In short, I could say that all the meditations are directed toward helping us to release those kinds of tensions inside us. I think that the meditation for such a hurt could be concentration on the fact of impermanence and knowing it cannot go on much longer. Maybe that person did not mean to hurt even though I perceive it as a hurt. I think the meditation on impermanence would be most effective.

Q. The same way with anger, too?

A. In another way, that hurt which we hold inside is also a form of a grudge. That is one aspect of a grudge, right? So when we release that grudge, we see that it served no purpose. If we can look at the useless-ness of the grudge itself, then I think that could be helpful. For instance, if you are hurt in that manner and you return the hurt, it will still not go away. Returning the same kind of deed does not help. Also, if you cling to a hurt, then you are hurting yourself again and again, reliving the same incident. You are not letting go of it. Just staying within that state is really destructive to yourself, as well as to whoever has hurt you. That makes it more intense. So thinking about those aspects and just trying to be a little bit logical, we may be able to let go of that grudge, or make it a little less intense. Holding a grudge is another way of holding an illness inside us, which is not perceptible to anybody else. We are carrying a huge pain inside us, a pain invisible to anybody else's eyes, a pain which is very real inside our heart. That pain is too big a burden to carry around.

Q. Is it also our responsibility to give our acceptance to a person who loses their temper towards us? If they feel badly, should we help them in the same way to let them know that we did not take offense at their actions?

A. As I mentioned, if somebody uses very harsh words against you at some time, and you don't return them and instead, if you are able to smile at it, then suddenly that makes it less heavy for that person. That will reduce the whole intensity of the anger. For our part, it is a wonderful thing to be able to accept that kind of defeat gracefully because even though it is a defeat in that moment, in a true sense it is a victory on our part. In the *Eight Verses on Thought Training* by Langri Tangpa, it says, "To be able to accept a defeat on our part and offer the victory to the other is one of our practices."

Q. Geshe-la, how does a person of skilful means strike a balance between spending time with a person who is suffering and the time one should spend in seclusion concentrating strictly on one's practice?

A. I think there is a balance between spending your time in seclusion and being with a person who is very miserable. If being with that person can be helpful, and the decision is made purely out of compassion, I think certainly you should choose your compassion. However, if you really are trying to fulfill attachment in the guise of caring, you know, if your want is to be with that person because of some kind of attachment or longing, then certainly I think the choice of meditation is better. We have to make sure that our choice is done purely out of caring and compassion. Whereas if the choice is because of the thought, "If I were to serve that person, I would look a little better with my social life. Everyone will think better of me, or that will enhance my image, or I will be able to get some kind of inheritance from that person"—

if it is done with that kind of attitude, that kind of motive, certainly I would choose the meditation over that.

Q. If you forgive somebody who harms you terribly, why is it necessary for them to give you their negative karma also? Besides, you know that nobody can suffer somebody else's karma, so what is the purpose of someone's negative karma to follow you?

A. You are right. You forgive from your heart and you cannot accept or assume somebody's negative deeds and bear his or her burden yourself. But the reason why we choose to accept negative deeds on our part is that even though it is impossible to suffer another's karma, nevertheless, if it *were* possible to have such a capacity, then we would choose to have it. By choosing that we are learning to open our heart much more. We are learning to open our hearts further and to make more accommodations, making our heart stronger and much more forceful than it was before. So in essence, learning to accept certain things will enable us to be a much stronger person. For that reason, we ask to accept the negative karma of others.

Taking such steps leads us to liking the person whom we once perceived as an enemy. Eventually, we learn to care for that person far more than our own parents or best friends. We learn to treat them equally or even better than our relatives. We reach that point because this practice gives us the mental strength to do so. For that reason, Shantideva in the *Bodhicaryavatara* says, "May all the negativities of sentient beings mature upon me." We not only wish that mentally, but we wish that it would truly happen. We wish that all the negativities of every one of the sentient beings be matured upon us and that they become free of those negativities. By thinking this way, we develop and grow through these meditations. Of course the results of the karma which they contracted will mature on whomever has committed that karma.

In the Sutra itself, the Buddha says that the karma that is committed or collected by anybody will not mature on the earth or in the water, or in the wind, or in space, but will happen only to the person who has committed the cause for that karma. But even though that is a fact, just mentally wishing to take on others' negative karma can strengthen our mind. If we do these practices as mentioned, then certainly we can receive a tremendous benefit from this meditation. How effective the mind can become through further development and growth in mental strength will be evident later in your life.

# ▓ APPENDICES

Tonglen Practice

Outline of the Root Verses

*Serlingpa*

# ⠿ Tonglen Practice

## FIVE CATEGORIES OF TONGLEN
### Equality of Oneself and Others

THE FIRST TOPIC TO CONTEMPLATE is that we are all equal. This doesn't mean that we all have the same appearance, size or build. As explained in the Lama Chöpa (Guru Puja), all sentient beings are equal in that we all dislike even the least suffering, and we have an insatiable desire for happiness. The more happiness we have, the more we want. Realizing this, we should have the same concern for others as for ourselves and we should cherish them as we do ourselves.

When we start to practice this, we can first start with our spouse, our friend, or the people with whom we live. If we are able to equalize our concern for those beings with the concern we have for ourselves, then we can gradually expand the boundary of concern to our neighbors, and so forth.

### Disadvantages of Self-Cherishing

The second topic is the disadvantages of selfishness. We need to come to the realization that all the suffering and all the things that we dislike stem from selfishness or self-cherishing. For that reason, the Lama Chöpa likens self-cherishing to a chronic illness. In fact, it is far worse than the most contagious disease, because it serves as the cause of all undesired suffering and illness in our life. Whenever we experience suffering in the form of illness or negative situations, we should confront our own self-cherishing and say to ourselves, "You are responsible for all this suffering." Every single day we have to point the finger at our own self-cherishing and accept that it is responsible for all our suffering.

The grasping of ego, or self-cherishing, becomes one of the biggest monsters. We need to realize that it is our worst enemy and that it lives within us. So for that reason we need to work at finding some means of removing this enemy or bringing it under control.

It says in Shantideva's *Bodhicaryavatara* that all the suffering and predicaments in this world are the result of self-cherishing—of being concerned only for the happiness of ourselves and regarding ourselves as more precious than others. Conversely, Shantideva states in the last two lines of this verse that all the existing happiness in this world is the result of cherishing others. He says of the grasping of the ego, "What use is that monster in me?"

### The Benefits of Cherishing Others

Similarly, in his *Lama Chöpa*, Panchen Losang Chökyi Gyeltsen says, "The thought of cherishing others and wanting to lead them to happiness is the source of limitless realizations and great qualities." Therefore, even if the entire community of sentient beings arises as my enemy, in return may I be able to cherish every one of them in my own life. Similarly, verse six of the *Eight Verses on Thought Training* says, "When someone I have benefited and in whom I have placed great trust hurts me very badly, I will practice seeing that person as my supreme teacher."

In the *Seven Point Thought Training*, Geshe Chekawa encourages us to contemplate the kindness of all sentient beings and to remain grateful to them. Furthermore, Shantideva says, "I do not need to talk more about the benefits of cherishing others, because you can understand it by just comparing how much buddhas gain with how little we have achieved."

Shakyamuni Buddha started out equal to sentient beings, but because he had the capacity to care for others and developed bodhicitta, he achieved great enlightenment. Because we have not developed our capacities as Buddha did, we remain sentient beings unable to advance. In *Lama Chöpa* it says, "Ordinary sentient beings work only for themselves, whereas buddhas work for others." Through understanding this example, we gain the motivation to learn to exchange ourselves with others. The only difference between the *Lama Chöpa* and the *Bodhicaryavatara* is the words; the basic message is the same. Studying the different texts is extremely helpful, because it gives us different ways of looking at things and helps us to expand our understanding.

## Exchange of Self With Others

The fourth topic is the actual exchange of the self with others. What we must do here is to replace our previous self-cherishing thoughts with thoughts of cherishing others and ignore our own selfish concerns. Here is an illustration. If there are two mountains and we are on one of them, that one becomes our side; the second mountain becomes the other side. But if we are on the second mountain looking at the first mountain, the first one becomes the other side. So we have to change our point of reference regarding whom we cherish most. We need to change our perspective and replace our self-cherishing thoughts with thoughts of cherishing others.

## Giving and Receiving Meditation

The fifth topic is the practice of giving and receiving, or tonglen meditation. The four preceding topics come together in tonglen meditation practice.

## ACTUAL MEDITATION

### Visualize the Field of Merit

When we are in the proper physical position, we visualize the merit field. There are several types of merit field visualizations from the lamrim that we can do. Two are listed below: the first is a more extensive visualization for advanced students. The second visualization is abbreviated for beginning students or for advanced practitioners with limited time.

### Extensive Visualization

We visualize the merit field at eye level, in the space in front of us. In the center, we visualize a huge throne on top of which is a smaller throne and higher up in the center is our root guru and other gurus around him. We should visualize Shakyamuni Buddha as the principal figure of the merit field. To the right of Shakyamuni Buddha, we visualize Buddha Maitreya surrounded by the lamas of the expansive conduct lineage, i.e., the lamas of the path and stages. On the left of Shakyamuni Buddha, we visualize the Buddha Manjushri and gurus of the profound wisdom lineage. At the center, right behind and above him, we visualize the lineage gurus of blessed practices. In front of Shakyamuni Buddha, we visualize the root guru with all of the subsequent lineage gurus down to our present guru. They are all encircled by the meditational deities of the four classes of tantra.

Since there are countless meditational deities (*yidams*), we have to believe that the entire community of meditational deities is on that spot. We also need to visualize the presence of all of the one thousand buddhas of the fortunate era, including the eight medicine buddhas, thirty-five confession buddhas, and so forth. We have to feel the presence of all of the countless buddhas in the space in front of us. Just below the buddhas, we visualize the presence of the bodhisattvas. We must be as imaginative as possible so that we feel the presence of limitless numbers of bodhisattvas. Below them we visualize the presence of arhats and arya beings, of the pratyekabuddhas and shravakas. Just below them, we visualize the presence of all the dakas and dakinis, including all the dakas and dakinis who are beyond the world. The bottom row is encircled by all the dharmapalas, including those that are beyond the world such as six-armed Mahakala, Kalarupa, and so on. We have to believe very strongly that the presence of all these beings is like the constellations of stars in the sky.

## Abbreviated Visualization

We visualize the Buddha at eye level, two arm-lengths away, seated on a large golden throne. The throne is adorned with precious jewels and supported at each of the four corners by a pair of snow lions. His seat consists of a large open lotus on top of which rest two radiant discs— a white moon disc, and a golden sun disc—resting one on top of the other. These three objects represent the three principal realizations of the path to great enlightenment: the lotus, renunciation or compassion; the sun, emptiness; and the moon, bodhicitta.

Buddha is seated in the full-lotus posture smiling beautifully at all beings. He is clad in saffron-colored robes and radiating golden light. The palm of his right hand rests on his right knee. His left hand holds a bowl filled with nectar resting in his lap. The nectar represents the teachings that cure our deluded states of mind.

Buddha's loving compassionate gaze looks at each of us with total acceptance free of judgment and favoritism. His whole being radiates love and omniscience streaming from his heart to ours. These rays fill us with courage and strength to successfully complete the practice of giving and receiving. It is important for us to keep in mind the inseparability of the Buddha and our guru.

## Visualizing the Field of Sentient Beings

After we have visualized the object of refuge or the merit field, we need to envision our own father on our right, and our own mother on our left. Immediately behind us, we visualize all our relatives, siblings, and good friends. Immediately in front of us, we should visualize our worst enemies or those we simply don't like, as well as animals we fear such as snakes, birds, scorpions, etc. In short, we need to imagine very strongly the entire community of sentient beings in the six realms all around us. But we should visualize them all in the form of human beings who are experiencing internally the respective suffering of the particular realm they belong to, like the hell realm, etc. That is how we should imagine them—all undergoing the most unbearable suffering of their particular place but externally in the form of human beings. Just the sight of these beings should help produce a strong, forceful compassion inside of us. And in the center we should make a very strong and forceful wish for the immediate end to their suffering. More than that, we need to make a very strong wish to remove all the causes of suffering. We should think, "How wonderful it would be if we could remove their negative mental states and bad actions." By thinking more about this, we develop stronger compassion (removing suffering from all others) and loving kindness (giving happiness to all others).

## Visualizing the Six Realms

The six realms are representations of our own mental afflictions and the resultant suffering. Each realm has its own level of suffering proportional to its causes. The first three realms are referred to as the lower realms and the last three, the upper realms. All these realms are the result of our karma: the three lower realms are the result of bad karma. The three upper realms are the result of good karma. A brief description of the six realms and some specific causes are as follows.

1. *The Hell Realm:* The most oppressive is the unbearable torture by heat. The suffering of cold hell is intolerable freezing. In another section of the hell realm people hit one another with weapons and the body is severed into thousands of pieces. The general cause of entering a hell realm is hatred and anger.

2. *Hungry Ghost Realm:* Hungry ghosts undergo severe hunger and thirst. The root cause of their predicament is miserliness or selfishness.

3. *Animal Realm:* The beings in this realm suffer from sickness and death, hunger, thirst, heat, cold, the continuous fear of being devoured, and extreme stupidity. The primary cause of their malaise is ignorance.

4. *Human Realm:* The primary difficulties experienced in the human realm are birth, illness, aging and death. In addition, suffering is caused by fighting between nations, neighbors and individuals. In some places, people experience hunger and lack of shelter. If we want to look deeper into the tremendous amount of suffering we just have to look at the newspaper, radio or television. The causes of all human difficulties are attachment, anger and ignorance.

5. *Asura (Demigod) Realm:* The demigods, even though they are good looking and their existence is relatively trouble-free, suffer severe anguish—fighting with each other and with the gods—attempting to reach the more bountiful god realm. The cause of their troubles is a result of jealousy.

6. *Deva (Celestial God) Realm:* The devas have a good life, with everything they could ask for. Before they die, however, they receive a premonition of their death and their next place of birth. The deterioration of their body is slow and painful. The cause of their sorrow is the result of pride.

The more deeply we think about the individual suffering of the six realms and its causes, the stronger will be our compassion and our desire to attain enlightenment.

## THE TECHNIQUE

We will broadly cover the technique of how to conduct our meditation of tonglen (giving and receiving). Of all the practices we can do, this is one of the most important. If we can do this in our daily practice, it will prove to be an indispensable tool.

In the meditation on tonglen, we should concentrate on people who are oppressed by suffering, seriously ill, mentally disturbed, poor, downtrodden, social outcasts, or otherwise experiencing difficulties. Focus primarily on these people but also include all beings.

### Receiving

We need to visualize all sentient beings surrounding us. We receive from them their sufferings and negativities in the form of dark-colored rays which ooze out of these beings and come towards us.

These rays represent three things: 1) their suffering; 2) the source of their suffering—their karma and negative mental states; and 3) their delusions or obscurations that block the understanding of or direct insight into all things. These three constitute all the problems that sentient beings experience, including their suffering, quarrels, dissatisfactions, and so on.

We should visualize dark rays coming from every sentient being just as we see vapor coming from the damp ground on a hot day. We need to visualize the dark rays as suffering from the sentient beings of the six realms—from the hell beings, from the hungry ghosts, animals, humans, asuras, and devas. These rays collectively join together, gather strength, and build up energy like a small cloud. We visualize this potent, highly concentrated black cloud in front of us, while we hold it there for a moment. At the center of our heart, we visualize a black bubble representing our illnesses, suffering, negative karmas and negative mental states and, most importantly, our self-cherishing. Inhaling this externally concentrated, smoke-colored black cloud through our nose, the dark mass drops on top of the visualized internal black bubble located inside our heart. These dissolve into each other to become completely destroyed and disappear. When we are through with this, we should have an immense sense of purification and relief. We should think that we have mentally purified all sentient beings and have placed them in a state of peace. We should now visualize a fault-free society: where there is no one in hospitals, the blind can see, the deaf can hear, and true peace prevails.

*Giving*

Next, we send out white rays of light representing the essence of our body, wealth and merit. Emanating from our heart, the rays touch all sentient beings, and transform them according to their present need. So those who desperately need medicine receive medicine; those who need clothes receive clothes—whatever they need at that moment they receive. The white light, originating from our heart, is exhaled out through the nose, and saturates the entire space, instantaneously satisfying the needs of every sentient being. This is one way of visualizing tonglen, the practice of giving and receiving.

When we finish such a meditation, we should reflect on the fact that the meditator, the meditation, and the object of our meditation are all empty of inherent existence.

# ⦙ Outline of the Root Verses

## EIGHT VERSES ON THOUGHT TRAINING

1. Seeking Enlightenment to Benefit Others and Holding Others as Dear
2. Seeing Others as Supreme
3. Preventing Delusions
4. Holding Difficult People as Dear
5. Accepting Defeat
6. Regarding Those Who Harm Us as a Teacher
7. Exchange of Self with Others
8. Seeing All Things as Illusion

## THE THIRTY-SEVEN BODHISATTVA PRACTICES

Supplication
Author's Pledge

1. Enthusiastic Perseverance
2. Abandoning the Birthplace
3. Being Free from Distractions
4. Abandoning Preoccupation with this Life
5. Avoiding Evil Friends
6. Treasuring the Spiritual Friend
7. Taking Refuge
8. Refraining from Negative Deeds

# Glossary

Skt. = Sanskrit

Tib. = Tibetan

*arhat* (Skt.). One who has gone beyond rebirth in cyclic existence.

*arya* (Skt.). Noble being or saint; one who has realized the path of direct insight into the way things truly exist.

*Asanga* (5th c.). Indian scholar who founded the Cittamatra or Mind-Only school.

*Atisha* (982-1054). Indian mahasiddha who revitalized Buddhism in Tibet and founded the Kadam tradition. Author of *Lamp for the Path to Enlightenment*.

*Avalokiteshvara* (Skt.). Male meditational deity embodying fully enlightened compassion. Often pictured with 1,000 arms.

*enlightenment* (Skt. *bodhi*). Full enlightenment; buddhahood; the ultimate goal of Buddhist practice, attained when all limitations have been removed from the mind and all one's positive potential has been realized; a state characterized by unlimited compassion, skill and wisdom.

*bhikshu* (Skt.). A male renunciant in the Buddhist order; monk.

*bhikshuni* (Skt.). A female renunciant in the Buddhist order; nun.

*bhumi* (Skt.). Literally, ground; level on the bodhisattva path

*bodhicitta* (Skt.). The "thought of enlightenment"; the determination to attain enlightenment for the benefit of sentient beings. There are two types: relative and ultimate. Relative bodhicitta is further classified into two types: aspiring and engaging bodhicitta.

*bodhisattva* (Skt.). One who truly generates bodhicitta.

*buddha* (Skt.). Enlightened or fully awakened one; a being who has completely abandoned all obscurations and has perfected every good quality.

*buddhas' children.* Heirs of the buddhas; those who will inherit buddhahood; bodhisattvas.

*calm-abiding.* A meditative state of one-pointed focus; quietude.

*cause and effect.* See *karma.*

*celestial god* (Skt. *deva*). A type of being who enjoys the highest pleasures to be found in cyclic existence but who is afflicted with pride.

*Chenrezig.* Tibetan name for Avalokiteshvara.

*cyclic existence.* See *samsara.*

*dakas and dakinis* (Skt.). Male and female Buddhist yogis who have achieved high realizations on the tantric path.

*Dalai Lama.* The temporal and spiritual leader of Tibet, recognized as the human embodiment of Avalokiteshvara, the bodhisattva of compassion.

*demi-god.* A type of being who enjoys great comfort and pleasure, but still suffers from jealousy and quarreling.

*desire realm.* Lowest of the three main divisions of samsara; the desire realm is further subdivided into six realms, including the hell realm, animal realms; and human realm.

*deva* (Skt.). See *celestial god.*

*dharma* (Skt.). The teachings of the Buddha; that which holds one back from suffering.

*dharmapalas* (Skt.). Dharma protectors; non-samsaric beings who have vowed to protect the dharma and its practitioners.

*Dromtönpa.* Tibetan scholar and main student of Atisha.

*emptiness.* See *shunyata*

*endowments.* There are ten endowments which enable us to practice dharma: 1) birth as a human being; 2) birth in a country where the opportunity to practice dharma exists; 3) sound body and mind; 4) birth into a life free from serious crime; 5) faith in Buddha's teaching; 6) presence of a spiritual master; 7) availability of the dharma; 8) the flourishing of the dharma; 9) fellowship of others who are following the teachings; and 10) exisitence of favorable conditions.

*exceptional thought.* The sixth step of the seven-step method for the cultivation of bodhicitta as taught by Maitreya and Arya Asanga: a special sympathy and enhanced desire for helping sentient beings.

*form realm.* Second of the three main divisions of samsara.

*formless realm.* Highest of the three main divisions of samsara.

*freedoms.* There are eight freedoms conducive to the practice of dharma. These freedoms are 1) not being born as a hell-being; 2) not being born as a hungry ghost; 3) not being born as an animal; 4) not being born as a god; 5) not being born in a place where there is no dharma; 6) being free from perverted views; 7) being free from deluded practices; and 8) being free from stupidity.

*geshe* (Tib.). Literally a "spiritual friend." In the Gelug tradition of Tibetan Buddhism, the title is used for one who has mastered the range of teachings on Buddhist philosophy and meditation practices.

*Geshe Chekawa.* Tibetan scholar of the Kadam tradition who wrote the *Seven Point Thought Training.*

*Geshe Langri Tangpa.* Tibetan scholar of the Kadam tradition who wrote the *Eight Verses on Thought Training.*

*great compassion.* The firm and spontaneous resolve to separate all sentient beings without exception from the suffering of cyclic existence.

*great love.* The firm and spontaneous resolve to endow all sentient beings without exception with the real, lasting happiness that knows no suffering.

*guru* (Skt.). A spiritual guide or teacher; translated in Tibetan as lama.

*Guru Puja* (Skt.). Offering ritual performed in honor of the spiritual masters; Tibetan text written by Panchen Lama Chökyi Gyeltsen.

*Hevajra* (Skt.). One of the Mahanuttarayoga tantras.

*higher realms.* See *six realms.*

*Hinayana* (Skt.). The "lesser vehicle" or "individual vehicle" as opposed to the "great vehicle" of the Mahayana. The practitioners on this vehicle strive for their own individual liberation, or the state of an arhat.

*hungry ghost.* A type of being who suffers from thirst and starvation; inhabitant of one of the lower realms.

*impermanence.* Concept that everything that has a cause is subject to change.

*jneyavarana* (Skt.). The obstructive aspect of the imprint of the afflictions that presents one from attaining the omniscient state of a buddha.

*Kadam.* Tradition of Tibetan Buddhism founded by Atisha.

*karma* (Skt.). Action; the working of cause and effect whereby positive actions produce happiness and negative actions produce suffering; the impression or seed that an action leaves on one's mental continuum, which must eventually ripen and produce a result.

*kleshavarana* (Skt.). The obstruction to liberation caused by negative mental states, or afflictions.

*lam-rim* (Tib.). "Stages of the Path to Enlightenment"; a reformulation of Shakyamuni Buddha's words into a complete and integrated system of practice, which outline the practices leading to great enlightenment.

*Lam-rim Chenmo* (Tib.). Lama Tsongkhapa's most extensive and in-depth *lam-rim* text, also known as the *Great Stages of the Path.*

*lama* (Tib.). Guru; spiritual teacher.

*Lama Chöpa* (Tib.). See *Guru Puja.*

*Lokeshvara* (Skt.). See *Avalokiteshvara.*

*lojong* (Tib.). Thought training.

*lower realms.* See *six realms.*

*mahaparinirvana* (Skt.). Great passing away from samsara.

*mahasiddha* (Skt.). A greatly accomplished tantric practitioner.

*Mahayana* (Skt.). The "great vehicle"; the path of those seeking enlightenment for the sake of benefiting others.

*Maitreya* (Skt.). The next founding buddha to come once Shakyamuni Buddha's teachings have disappeared from the world.

*mandala.* (Skt.). A symbolic representation of the universe; the abode of a meditational deity as the emanation of that deity; one's personal surroundings as a reflection of one's state of mind.

*Manjushri* (Skt.). Male meditational deity embodying fully enlightened wisdom.

*Mara* (Skt.). Demon; personified obstruction.

*method.* The techniques employed on the path to enlightenment, often conceived as the first five perfections.

*Milarepa* (1040-1123). Great Tibetan saint and chief disciple of Marpa.

*Mount Meru.* Giant mountain at the center of the world system and the mandala offering.

*naga* (Skt.). A half-human, half-dragon sentient being.

*Nagarjuna.* Indian mahasiddha who elucidated the Perfection of Wisdom Sutras of Shakyamuni Buddha and founded the Madhyamika school of philosophy.

*Nalanda.* A Buddhist university in ancient India.

*Naropa* (11th c.). A great Indian yogi, chief disciple of Tilopa and teacher of Marpa.

*negative acts.* Actions motivated by delusion which lead to suffering.

*nirvana* (Skt.). The state of complete liberation from samsara; the goal of the practitioner seeking his or her own freedom from suffering.

*omniscience.* The quality of a buddha's mind which signifies complete knowledge of all reality.

*paramita* (Skt.). See *perfections.*

*penetrating insight.* Insight into emptiness (*shunyata*).

*perfections.* The six "transcending" practices of the Mahayana path, which define the bodhisattva's way of life: 1) generosity; 2) ethics; 3) patience; 4) enthusiastic perseverance; 5) concentration; 6) wisdom.

*Prajnaparamita Sutra* (Skt.). The *Perfection of Wisdom Sutra.*

*Pratimoksha Sutra* (Skt.). "The code of individual liberation"; the precepts for Buddhist monks and nuns in the discipline section of the scriptures.

*pratyekabudhha* (Skt.). "Solitary realizer"; higher of the two types of Hinayana arhats, who attains nirvana without needing teachings in that lifetime, but lacks the complete realization of a buddha and thus cannot help other sentient beings as much as a buddha can.

*rebirth.* The entrance of consciousness into a new state of existence after death; a process over which deluded sentient beings have no control.

*refuge.* The attitude of relying upon someone or something for guidance and help; in Buddhism one takes refuge in the Three Jewels or three sublime ones: the Buddha, the Dharma, and the Sangha.

*relative bodhicitta.* The altruistic aspiration to attain full enlightenment based on boundless compassion for all living beings; an actual engaging in meditation practice in order to attain this state and to have the means of fully benefiting others. See *bodhicitta.*

*Shakyamuni Buddha* (563-483 BC). Fourth of the 1000 founding buddhas of this present world age; born a prince of the Shakya clan in North India; founder of what came to be known as Buddhism.

*Sakya Pandita* (1187-1251). Great meditator and scholar of the Sakya order. Considered to be an emanation of Manjushri, the bodhisattva of wisdom.

*shamatha* (Skt.). See *calm abiding*.

*samadhi* (Skt.). A profound meditative state in which the mind is fully concentrated on a single object.

*samsara* (Skt.). Cyclic existence; the recurring cycle of death and rebirth under the control of ignorance.

*Sangha* (Skt.). Monastic community following the teachings of the Buddha; the assembly of noble beings on the path to liberation and enlightenment; spiritual friends who help us in our practice of the dharma.

*Shantideva.* Indian scholar and yogi; author of the classic text, *Bodhicaryavatara.*

*self-cherishing.* The self-centered attitude of considering one's own happiness to be more important than that of others; the main obstacle to be overcome in the development of bodhicitta.

*sentient being.* Any being having a consciousness who has not yet attained buddhahood.

*Serlingpa* (10th c.). Atisha's guru; authority on bodhicitta who is believed to have lived on the "golden island" of Sumatra in Indonesia.

*six realms.* States of existence within samsara consisting of the three lower realms and the three higher realms. The three lower realms are hell, hungry ghost, and animal. The three higher realms are human, demigod, and celestial god.

*spiritual friend.* See *geshe*.

*spiritual master.* See *guru*.

*shravaka* (Skt.). Literally "hearer" or "listener"; one who has achieved liberation from cyclic existence on the Hinayana path mainly with the help of a spiritual guide.

*shunyata* (Skt.). Voidness or emptiness; the absence of any independent, self-existence in persons or things.

*supreme community.* See *Sangha*.

*sutra* (Skt.). A discourse of Shakyamuni Buddha; the pre-tantric division of Buddhist teachings stressing the scriptural texts and the teachings they contain.

*Sutrayana.* Vehicle of the sutra teachings.

*tantra* (Skt.). Literally "thread" or "continuity"; practices involving identification of oneself with a fully enlightened deity; esoteric practices not taught in the sutras.

*tathagata* (Skt.). A buddha, a perfectly realized one.

*three doors.* Body, speech, and mind.

*three times.* Past, present, and future.

*tonglen* (Tib.). Literally "giving and receiving"; the meditation on receiving the suffering of others and giving them happiness.

*Tsongkhapa, Lama* (1357-1419). Founder of the Gelug tradition of Tibetan Buddhism; revitalized many Sutra and Tantra lineages as well as the monastic tradition in Tibet. He wrote *The Great Stages of the Path* using Atisha's *Lamp for the Path* as his root text.

*ultimate bodhicitta.* The experiential realization that all beings and objects are naturally empty of inherent, independent existence. See *bodhicitta.*

*Vajrapani* (Skt.). Wrathful male meditational deity embodying Buddha's power.

*Vasubandhu.* Indian scholar and author of *Abhidharmakosha.*

*Vikramalashila.* A Buddhist university in ancient India.

*virtuous acts.* Positive actions which result in happiness.

*wish-granting gem.* A mythical jewel which will grant any wish

*yana* (Skt.). Literally "vehicle"; any path to enlightenment.

*yoga* (Skt.). Literally "union" or "yoke"; the spiritual discipline to which one adheres.

*yogi* (Skt.). A male practitioner of yoga; a tanric adept.

*yogini* (Skt.). A female practitioner of yoga; a tantric adept.

# Bibliography

Chandrakirti, *Madhyamakavatara* (*Guide to the Middle Way*). Translated by C.W. Huntington in *The Emptiness of Emptiness*. Honolulu: The University of Hawaii Press, 1989.

Chekawa, Geshe. *Lojong Dondunma*. (*The Seven Point Thought Transformation*). Translated by Brian Beresford with Gonsar Tulku and Sharpa Tulku in Geshe Rabten and Geshe Dhargyey's *Advice from a Spiritual Friend.*, Boston: Wisdom Publications, 1996.

Conze, Edward, trans. *The Large Sutra on Perfect Wisdom*. Berkeley: University of California Press, 1975.

Conze, Edward, trans. *The Perfection of Wisdom in Eight Thousand Lines and its Verse Summary*. Bolinas: Four Seasons Foundation, 1973.

Dharmarakshita. *Tegpa Chenpo Lojong Tsoncha Khorlo* (*The Wheel of Sharp Weapons*). Translation and commentary by Geshe Ngawang Dhargyey, et al., in *The Wheel of Sharp Weapons*, Dharamsala: Library of Tibetan Works and Archives, 1973.

First Dalai Lama. "*White Cloud on the Tip of the Mountain.*" In *Bridging the Sutras and Tantras*, Chapter IV: "Song of the Eastern Snow Mountains" Compiled and translated by Glenn H. Mullin. Ithaca: Gabriel/Snow Lion, 1981,1982.

Langri Tangpa, Geshe. *Lojong Tsigyema* (*Eight Verses on Thought Training*). Translated in *Kindness, Clarity and Insight* by Fourteenth Dalai Lama by Jeffrey Hopkins. Ithaca; Snowlion, 1984.

Translated in the Fourteenth Dalai Lama's, *Four Essential Buddhist Commentaries*, Dharamsala: Library of Tibetan Works and Archives, 1982.

Maitreya. *Abhisamayalamkara* (*Ornament of Clear Realizations*). Translated by Edward Conze. Rome: Instituto per il Medio ed Estremo Oriente, 1954.

Nagarjuna. *Rajaparikatha-ratnamala* in *The Precious Garland and the Song of the Four Mindfulnesses*. Translated and edited by Jeffrey Hopkins. New York: Harper and Row, 1975.

Nagarjuna. *Suhrllekha* (Letter to a Friend). *Nagarjuna's Letter* Translated by Geshe Lobsang Tharchin and Artemus B. Engle. Dharamsala: Library of Tibetan Works and Archives, 1979.

Ngawang Dhargyey, Geshe. *An Anthology of Well-Spoken Advice: On the Graded Paths of the Mind*. Edited by Alexander Berzin. Translated by Sharpa Tulku. Dharamsala: Library of Tibetan Works and Archives, 1982.

Ngawang Dhargyey, Geshe. *Tibetan Tradition of Mental Development*. Dharamsala: Library of Tibetan Works and Archives, 1974.

Panchen Lama Losang Chökyi Gyeltsen. *La-ma Chos-pa (Guru Puja)*. Translated by Alex Berzin, et al. Dharamsala: Library of Tibetan Works and Archives, 1979, 1981, 1982.

Rabten, Geshe. *Echoes of Voidness*. London: Wisdom, 1983.

Rabten, Geshe. *The Essential Nectar: Meditations on the Buddhist Path*. Edited and translated by Martin Willson. London: Wisdom, 1984.

Tenzin Gyatso, the Fourteenth Dalai Lama. *The Union of Bliss and Emptiness: A Commentary on the Lama Chöpa Guru Yoga Practice*. Translated by Thupten Jinpa. Ithaca: Snow Lion, 1988.

Togmay Zangpo. *Gyal-sras Lag-len So-dun-ma (Thirty-seven Practices of the Bodhisattvas)*. Translated in the Fourteenth Dalai Lama's, *Four Essential Buddhist Commentaries*. Dharamsala: Library of Tibetan Works and Archives, 1982.

Tsongkhapa. *Lam-rim Chenmo (Great Exposition of the Stages of the Path)*.

Vasubandhu. *Abhidharmakosha (Treasury of Knowledge)*. French translation, 6 tomes by Louis de La Vallee Poussin. Paris: 1923-31.

Shantideva. *Bodhisattvacaryavatara (Guide to the Bodhisattva's Way of Life)*. Translated by Stephen Batchelor. Dharamsala: Library of Tibetan Works and Archives, 1979.

# About the Author

GESHE TSULTIM GYELTSEN was born in 1924 in the Kham province of eastern Tibet. His parents named him Jamphel Yeshe and at a young age he was inspired by the example of his uncle who was a monk at the local monastery. When the boy was only seven, he and his family decided that he would enter monastic life. For nine years he studied Sutra and Tantra and received teachings on dialectics under the tutelage of Geshe Jampa Thaye, a highly respected teacher from Sera Monastery.

When he was sixteen, Geshe Gyeltsen decided to continue his studies and left for Lhasa, the capital of Tibet, to study for his geshe degree at Sera Monastery. The geshe degree in the Gelug school is comparable to a western doctorate in Buddhist philosophy. The difference is that a geshe degree usually takes more than twenty years to complete.

Geshe Gyeltsen set out on the thirty-three day trek across twenty-five mountain passes, the only monk in a party of fifteen merchants and pilgrims. Near Lhasa, they stopped near Gaden Monastery where some monks invited him for tea the following day. The next morning as he climbed the hill toward Gaden, he saw the great monastery for the first time looking as though it would touch the sky. He wept tears of joy and knew without question that it was here, and not Sera, where he would continue his studies. That day was the anniversary of Lama Tsongkhapa's enlightenment. In the evening, the light offerings of butter lamps and the sound of chanting filled every room in the monastery and Geshe Gyeltsen felt deeply moved by its spiritual atmosphere.

He joined Shartse College, one of Gaden's two main colleges. The abbot at that time was the late Kyabje Zong Rinpoche who took a special interest in the young monk's progress. Geshe Gyeltsen studied logic, wisdom, compassion, ethics, phenomenology and mind training at Gaden for twenty years and later became a teacher of junior monks.

After the Tibetan Uprising of March 10th, 1959, word reached Gaden that His Holiness the Dalai Lama had left Tibet. Geshe Gyeltsen and a group of six other monks left the monastery after evening prayers and made their way to India across the Himalayas; members of a mass exodus fleeing the oppression of the Chinese Communist occupation. He was one of the few senior monks who managed to escape out of the twenty thousand monks that had lived at Gaden, Sera, and Drepung; Tibet's three largest monasteries.

Geshe Gyeltsen, with fifty of the most highly regarded monks from each monastery, resettled at Dalhousie in northern India where he studied for two more years before taking his final geshe examinations. These exams were attended by masters from all schools of Tibetan Buddhism. The last week of his exams took place in Dharamsala where Geshe Gyeltsen engaged in rigorous debates under the scrutiny of His Holiness the Dalai Lama and his two senior tutors, the late Kyabje Ling Rinpoche and the late Kyabje Trijang Rinpoche. He passed with honors and was awarded the highest degree of Lharampa Geshe.

In 1963, Geshe Gyeltsen traveled to Sussex, England, to teach at the Pestalozzi International Children's Village. He arrived with twenty-two Tibetan children who were mostly orphans or the children of parents still living in Tibet. For seven years he instructed these children in Tibetan writing, grammar, culture and Buddhist philosophy.

Geshe Gyeltsen came to the United States in 1976 and briefly held positions at USC, at UC Santa Barbara, and at UCLA where he taught meditation and Tibetan language. His university students requested that he start a teaching center, and in 1978 he founded a center for the study of Buddhism in Los Angeles.

Geshe Gyeltsen requested His Holiness the Dalai Lama to name the center and His Holiness gave the name of Thubten Dhargye Ling, which means Land of Flourishing Dharma. Thubten Dhargye Ling is now based in Long Beach where Geshe Gyeltsen offers classes in meditation, holds retreats, celebrates religious holidays, and gives regular teachings from traditional Buddhist texts. His teachings are archived on the Internet and are broadcast live over the web at tdling.com.

Geshe Gyeltsen is the author of *Keys to Great Enlightenment, Mirror of Wisdom* and *The Foundation of All Good Qualities*. He has founded centers in Northern California, Colorado, Texas, Mexico City and Denmark, and has students based around the world. He is also involved in various humanitarian projects in India, including the construction of an Indian School for the Blind, a new classroom and playground for an Indian school, and a home for Gaden Monastery's elderly monks. He also funds a Tibetan Elders Home, provides meals for schoolchildren, and helps to train Tibetan educators. He actively works for human rights and true autonomy for the Tibetan people.

Geshe Gyeltsen is known for his great compassion and personal warmth while retaining a traditional and uncompromising approach to teaching the dharma. His strength of vision and devotion to his practice transcend time and culture, and he continues to inspire his students with the legacy he has brought from Tibet.

Other books by Geshe Tsultim Gyeltsen:
*Mirror of Wisdom: Teachings on Emptiness* (TDL Publications, 2000)
*The Foundation of All Good Qualities: A Commentary on the Verses of Lama Tsongkhapa* (TDL Publications, 2006)

Other TDL books:
*Illuminating the Path to Enlightenemnt* by His Holiness the Dalai Lama (TDL Publications, 2002)

Interested persons may contact Thubten Dhargye Ling by calling (562) 621-9865, emailing office@tdling.com, or by writing to 3500 East 4th St. Long Beach, CA 90814. Visit the website at tdling.com.

### Geshe Langri Tangpa (1054—1123)
Author of *Eight Verses on Thought Training*
The thought training system of dharma practice contains one of the two main methods for developing bodhicitta. For a long time, however, they were kept secret as it was felt that people would not understand them. It wasn't until the great Kadampa geshe, Langri Tangpa, composed *Eight Verses on Thought Training* that these teachings became widely available and people were able to learn and practice them. Geshe Langri Tangpa received these teachings from Dromtönpa, who himself received them from the Indian master, Atisha, who brought them to Tibet.

TOGMEY ZANGPO (1295—1369)
Author of *The Thirty-Seven Bodhisattva Practices*
From an early age, Togmey Zangpo was known for being mostly concerned with helping others. Eventually, he became a monk and studied with various masters, becoming a very learned and realized practitioner. He was most famous for developing bodhichitta—the aspiration to seek enlightenment for the welfare of all sentient beings. He achieved this mainly through the thought training methods brought to Tibet by the Indian master, Atisha. Bodhicitta is the essential aspect of a bodhisattva, one who has developed the spontaneous altruistic determination to benefit others.

LOSANG GYALTSEN translated Geshe Gyeltsen's oral commentaries of these texts from Tibetan into English. Losang Gyaltsen is a graduate of Sanskrit University's Institute of Higher Tibetan Studies in Varanasi, India, and has worked as a translator for the Library of Tibetan Works and Archives.

## A Note About Dharma Books

Books containing dharma teachings or the images of dharma teachers are very precious because they represent the teachings and beings that can lead us to full enlightenment. This is a reason to treat dharma books with respect. According to tradition, we do not put dharma books, or any other dharma literature, on the floor or underneath other things, step over or sit on them, or use them for mundane purposes. They are kept in a clean, high place, separate from worldly writings.